Mitra-Varuna

Translated by Derek Coltman

Mitra-Varuna

An Essay on Two Indo-European Representations of Sovereignty

Georges Dumézil

ZONE BOOKS · NEW YORK

1988

ZONE BOOKS
611 Broadway, Suite 608
New York, NY 10012

Third printing 1996

Printed in the United States of America

Distributed by The MIT Press,
Cambridge, Massachusetts, and London, England

Library of Congress Cataloging-in-Publication Data

Dumézil, Georges, 1898–1986
[Mitra-Varuna. English]
Mitra-Varuna: an essay on two Indo-European representations / Georges Dumézil; translated by Derek Coltman.
p. cm.
Bibliography: p.
ISBN 0-942299-13-2 (pbk.)
1. Mythology, Indo-European. 2. Gods–Comparative studies. I. Title.
BL660.D813 1988 87-34052
291.1'3–dc19 CIP

To my teachers
Marcel Mauss and Marcel Granet

Contents

Preface to the Second Edition

The first edition of this work, which was published in May 1940, formed Volume LVI of the *Bibliothèque de l'Ecole des Hautes Etudes, Section des Religieuses.* The printing was a very small one, and soon exhausted. In my mind, however, *Mitra-Varuṇa* was to be merely the first in a series of studies devoted to a comparative exploration of the religions of Indo-European peoples, to the ideas those peoples had formed of human and divine society, and to a social and cosmic hierarchy in which Mitra and Varuṇa occupy only the uppermost level. Despite historical circumstances, this sequence of studies did in fact appear, at regular intervals, from 1941 through 1947, thanks to the devotion of Monsieur Gallimard and to that of my lifelong friend, Brice Parain. Today, however, those works find themselves severed from their roots, as it were, since many English-speaking, Scandinavian, and even French readers, unable to refer to the 1940 edition, must experience some uncertainty with regard to certain essential points in my arguments. A second edition therefore seems necessary.

It contains few changes. Material errors have been corrected, some paragraphs removed or changed, facts clarified. These revisions have been most extensive in the eighth section of Chapter Nine ("Nuada and Lug," titled "Nuada and Balor" in the first edition), which has been entirely rewritten and given a different thrust, and in several pages of the conclusion. I have also added to my notes a large number of references to books I wrote after *Mitra-Varuṇa*, which have made use of, clarified, or corrected some of its arguments. (The reference code, designed to facilitate the printer's task, is: *JMQ I* = *Jupiter-Mars-Quirinus*, 1941; *Horace et les Curiaces*, 1942; *Servius et la Fortune*, 1943; *JMQ II* = *Naissance de Rome*, 1944; *JMQ III* = *Naissance d'Archanges*, 1945; *Tarpeia*, 1947.)

There has been occasional criticism – some of it meant kindly, some not – of the decision I made over ten years ago to publish in this fragmentary fashion a work whose overall configuration and final conclusions still remain to be fixed. To some, the trust thus required of the reader betrayed a lack of either discretion or patience on my part. Others warned me that I was risking repetitions, regrets, and all sorts of awkwardnesses that would produce an extremely bad effect. Still others suggested that I was simply leaving room for subsequent, and possibly fraudulent, maneuvering. It was felt, in short, that I would find it easier to convince my readers if I presented them with my work at a later stage, finished, coordinated, and fully equipped with all its offensive and defensive weapons, rather than associating them with the hesitant process of my research. Nevertheless, I am persisting in my original plan, and for three reasons. First, the longer the work goes on, the further off the moment of a harmonious and satisfying synthesis appears. The next generation of workers in this field might be in a position to attempt this, but I know only too well that I shall no more have completed even a first exploration of this domain in ten years' time than I have today, since the area to be covered is the whole vast province of Eurasian prehistory, and the research needed must necessarily be based on a massive quantity of very diverse material. Second, I have found that this fragmentary form of publication is of use to me personally: at each stage, criticism and discussion have kept a tight rein (or so at least I hope) on the part played by arbitrary inventions or fixed ideas, both dangers of which I am well aware, but against which external control alone can prevail. Finally, we live in an age unfavorable to grand designs. In the course of what was once referred to as a lifetime, one's work is repeatedly at risk of being interrupted and destroyed. Cities and libraries disappear. University professors, as well as mothers and children, are lost in the tidal waves of deportation or the ashes of an oven; or else evaporate, along with bonzes and chrysanthemums, into dangerous corpuscles. The little each of us discovers therefore ought to be paid into the common account of human knowledge without too much delay, without any thought of first amassing a great treasure.

As for the methods, both comparative and analytic, that I am attempting to employ and also to perfect, there is little more to be said than can be found in the prefaces to my most recent books. One common – and very present – weakness of sociological work is multiplying preliminary rules and *a priori* definitions from which it later becomes impossible to break free; another is drawing up dazzling programs that one is prevented from fulfilling. As a consequence, many hours of work are lost each year in facile and flattering speculations that eventually prove somewhat unfruitful, at least from an intellectual point of view. I shall not add to this mental frittering.

From the two masters to whom this book is dedicated, I learned, among other things, a respect for the concrete and for the ever-changing material of one's studies. For, despite unjust criticism, nothing was more foreign to the thinking of those two great men than apriorism and exclusivism. Marcel Mauss once said to us, "I call sociology all science that has been done well"; and none of us has forgotten Marcel Granet's quip about the art of making discoveries: "Method is the *path, after* one has been along it." This does not mean that I have no conscious method. But to do is better than to preach. In young fields of study, whether comparative or otherwise, isn't everything ultimately governed by those classic rules of Descartes and John Stuart Mill, the rules of common sense? To make use of all the material that offers itself, no matter which particular disciplines share it for the moment, and without subjecting it to arbitrary categorizations of one's own; to examine what is given at length, with all its obvious facts, which are often less than facts, and also its mirages, which are sometimes more than mirages; to be wary of traditional opinions but also, and equally, of outlandish opinions and fashionable novelties; to avoid trammeling oneself with premature technical language; to regard neither boldness nor prudence as "the" virtue above all others, but to make use of both while continually checking the legitimacy of each step and the harmony of the whole. This "pentalogue" contains everything essential.

The most useful thing I can do here is to recount the various stages that make up the labor which has preoccupied me for almost a quarter-century. I embarked upon the comparative study of Indo-European religions at an extremely early age, with many illusions and ambitions in my baggage and, of course, without sufficient philological preparation. To cap that misfortune, the subject I first encountered, in 1924, was among the most wide-ranging and complex: *Le Festin d'immortalité*. In 1929, with the Indian Gandharva, the Greek centaurs, and the Roman Luperci, I found myself tackling a topic more amenable to definition and interpretation; but I was still unable to confine myself to the essential thrust of the facts or to the truly telling and useful parts of my exegesis. Yet I regret nothing, not even those early errors, those first tentative gropings. If at the outset, before attempting to wrestle directly with the new type of problems I had glimpsed, I had aimed at mastering any particular philology, the central focus of my thinking soon would have been displaced, and I should have merely become a more-or-less respectable specialist in the Roman, Greek or Indian field. But I felt that the undertaking was worth the effort, and that my tasks were to improve my knowledge of three or four domains simultaneously (always in particular relation to the same type of problems), and to keep my sights fixed "between" those specialities, at the probable point of their convergence. In this way, I hoped to achieve a kind of mental accommodation that would enable me, eventually, to whittle a somewhat too-inclusive interpretation down to a more precise, austere and objective analysis.

In 1930 the undertaking appeared to have foundered. One of my teachers, who had originally encouraged me without gauging any more clearly than I had the difficulties involved, was aware, above all, of the uncertainties apparent in my first two essays, as well as sensitive to the criticisms that certain young and brilliant flamines did not fail to make of my Lupercalia. Was I going to compromise the prestige of the entire comparative method that was then establishing itself with such acclaim in the linguistic field by employing it in a lateral, clumsy, perhaps illegitimate way? Fortunately, at that very moment, others came to understand the scope and richness of this field, and, to put it simply, they rescued me: Sylvain Lévi, Marcel Mauss and Marcel Granet were to be the guardian deities of this new discipline.

It was not until 1934, in a short study devoted to Uranos-Varuṇa, that I felt I had succeeded for the first time in dealing with a theme in the field of "comparative Indo-European religious studies" in a proper way, that is, in a very few pages aimed directly at the heart of the matter. That publication contained all the worthwhile results of the first lecture course I was asked to give, under the auspices of Sylvain Lévi, at the *Ecole des Hautes Etudes* in 1933-1934.

During the following years, I continued my attempts to deal with a series of precisely defined questions in the same way. Then, quite suddenly, during a lecture in the winter of 1937-1938, almost as a reward for so many failed but constantly renewed attempts, so much tentative but unremitting research, I glimpsed the fact that dominates and structures a large part of the material: the existence – at the very foundation of the ideology of most of the Indo-European peoples – of a tripartite conception of the world and society; a conception that is expressed, among the Arya of India and Iran, by a division into three classes (priests, warriors and herdsmen-cultivators) and, in Rome, by the most ancient triad of gods (Jupiter, Mars, Quirinus). During the next academic year (the last before the war), I used both my lecture courses to begin an investigation of the fundamental myths of the first and second cosmic and social "functions," which is to say, the myths of magical and juridical sovereignty and the myths of warrior-power or, to put it in Vedic terms, the myths of Mitra-Varuṇa and those of Indra-Vṛtrahan.

The first of those lecture courses provided the material for this book. The other, to which I have returned several times, has not yet provided results clear enough to permit the publication of anything other tnan fragments (specifically: *Vahagn* in *Revue de l'Histoire des Religions*, CXVII, 1938, p. 152ff.; *Deux traits du Tricéphale indo-iranien, ibid.*, CXX, 1939, p. 5ff.; *Horace et les Curiaces*, 1942); but I do not despair of succeeding fairly soon.

Since that time I have made every effort, no matter the topic, to highlight the numerous links that make it possible to keep one's bearing within the given religious structures, without falsifying their perspectives or proportions by emphasizing individual details. Hence my attempt, on two or three occasions, to deal with the most general problem, that of the underlying mythic and social structure of Jupiter-Mars-Quirinus. Hence, too, my somewhat unexpected discoveries relating to the origins of Roman "history" and to the field of Zoroastrian theology.

I shall always retain a particular fondness in my heart for the year 1938-1939; but it is a memory peopled by ghosts. Both at Sceaux and in Paris, Marcel Granet followed with his kindly eye the progress of an endeavor already so much in his debt. Every Thursday in the lecture hall, beside Roger Caillois, Lucien Gerschel and Elisabeth

Raucq, I would greet our gracious colleague Marie-Louise Sjoestedt, whose pupil in turn I became on Wednesdays when she taught me Welsh and Irish; she was not to survive France's first misfortunes. Pintelon, an assistant professor at the University of Ghent, was destined to perish in uniform while on guard in Belgium, even before the invasion. Deborah Lifschitz, from the Musée de l'Homme, so kind hearted and intelligent, was doomed to the horrors of Auschwitz. Other young faces were destined for other ordeals....

Georges Dumézil
Paris, January 1947

Preface to the First Edition

This essay investigates a certain bipartite conception of sovereignty that appears to have been present among the Indo-Europeans, and that dominated the mythologies of certain of the peoples who spoke Indo-European languages at the time of the earliest documents. In my earlier work, mostly devoted to the mechanisms and representations of sovereignty, I had already encountered some of the elements that interest me here; but I had previously understood their relations only very imperfectly. In this work, it is the broad system of those relations that I try to elucidate.

Let no one object, before reading this book, that it is always easy for a mind dialectically inclined to subject facts to a preconceived system. The system is truly inherent in the material. It may be observed, always the same, in the most diverse sets of facts – in all those sets of facts, one might say, that fall within the province of sovereignty. Further, it reveals regularly recurring links within those sets of facts that will provide the reader with a constant means of checking the probability of the whole and, should it be the case, of discerning any illusions or artifices on my part. In matters of pure speculation, coherence is merely one elementary quality of the reasoning required, and in no way a guarantee of truth. The same is not true, however, for the sciences of observation, where one is required to classify numerous and diverse objective data in accordance with their nature. I hope the reader will also take due note that, in the majority of the areas touched upon, there has been no need for me to reconstruct or to interpret anything whatsoever: those who used the myths, rituals and formulas were quite conscious of the system; my sole task has been to make clear its scope and its antiquity.

I trust, too, that there will be no complaint that I have exaggerated the clear-cut nature of the system. In practice, it is true, classifications are always less distinct than in theory, and one must be prepared to encounter a great many overlaps and compromises. But this conflict, if it is a conflict, is not between myself and the facts; it lies within the facts themselves, and is inherent in all human behavior: societies spend their time forming an ideal and simple conception of themselves, of their functioning, and sometimes of their mission, which they also constantly alter and make more complex.

Finally, let no one reproach me with having accorded excessive importance to elements that in later stages of a religion are secondary and, as it were, fossilized; it was precisely my task to throw some light upon the old and superseded states, by means of internal analysis and, above all, by the use of comparison. It is certainly true, for example, that as we approach the threshold of our own era, both the Luperci and flamines had lost almost all their importance in the life of the Roman state; the newly emerging empire was to prove grudging, indeed, in the status it granted to the former, and was not always able to find even a single candidate for the chief *flamonium*; but that in no way contradicts the fact that Rome's whole primitive "history" was built upon coupled notions, of which the Luperci and the flamines are merely the priestly expression.

I reproduce here, almost without alteration, a series of lectures given at the *Ecole des Hautes Etudes* in 1938-1939. I increasingly take the view that, given the field's present state of development, the comparatist shouldn't aspire to the "finish" rightly demanded of the philologist; that he should remain flexible, unanchored and ready to make good use of any criticism; that at all times he should keep firmly to the broad paths of the subject he is investigating and never lose sight of the general plan. I didn't even wish to burden myself with notes. Parentheses are sufficient for any references; discussions at the foot of one's pages are inappropriate in an exposition that is no more than a program.

The importance of the subject itself first became apparent to me in 1934, during a conversation with Sylvain Lévi. That great and kindly mind, having welcomed my *Ouranos-Varuṇa* had raised one question: "What about Mitra?" Early in 1938, during a Société Ernest Renan discussion of a paper in which I compared the Roman hierarchy of the three major flamines with the Brahmanic tripartition of society (see *Revue de l'Histoire des Religions*, CXVIII, 1938, pp. 188-200), Jean Bayet pointed out a similar difficulty relating to the actual title of the *flamen dialis*: "What about Dius Fidius?" The reader will soon perceive that these two questions are the whole question. The very fact that they occur symmetrically in India and in Rome, and in relation to divinities who are among the most archaic, led me to think that I was dealing, here again, not with a fortuitous coincidence, but with the vestiges of one of those religious mechanisms that are particularly well preserved in the extreme western and eastern reaches of the territory, among the Indo-Iranians, the Italiots and the Celts. My efforts have been directed at isolating that mechanism.

Naturally, I began by investigating Vedic India and Rome, since those two areas provided the first clues, and this constitutes the material in the first two chapters. By the end of Chapter Two, I was in a position to set out an exploratory program still confined to Rome, India and Iran; the next four chapters attempt to carry out this program. In Chapter Seven, certain reflections on the work accomplished thus far enabled me to move on to a set of homologous facts in the Germanic field; and those facts, partly because of their new form, posed a series of problems that had hitherto escaped me, and in which Rome, India and the Celtic world are all equally involved (Chapters Eight, Nine, Ten).

When this province of comparative mythology becomes better known, there may well be some advantage in following a different order, and, more particularly, in selecting a different starting point – just as textbooks in mathematical analysis dealing with, let us say, derived coefficients or imaginary numbers do not present the various parts of the theory in the same order as it was constructed historically, but move, as swiftly as possible, to its most convenient or most widely accepted points, so that their deductions may then proceed without hindrance over the same ground that early workers in the field had to toil over with such effort. We have not yet reached that stage; and it seemed to me more instructive to let my exposition follow the same paths as the original research. Constructive criticism will also be made easier by this method, to my great advantage. Indeed, criticism has provided me with powerful assistance already, during discussions with some of those present at the *Ecole des Hautes Etudes* when the lectures themselves were first delivered. It was Roger Caillois's criticisms that led to the observations in Chapter Eight; and it was Elisabeth Raucq, from the University of Ghent, who brought to my attention that Odhinn's mutilation could bear importantly on my subject (Chapter Nine). This trusting, generous and public collaboration is one of the characteristics and, I hasten to add, one of the privileges of our school, and it is with joy that I offer yet further testimony to it here.

I wish to thank Jules Bloch and Gabriel Le Bras, who were kind enough to read and improve this essay in manuscript, and Georges Deromieu, who helped me to revise the proofs.

G.D.

Paris, June 1939

Chapter I

Luperci and Flamines

In the course of earlier research I discovered a parallel between the rex-flamen dialis and the rāj(an)-brahman (*Flamen-Brahman, Annales du Musée Guimet, Bibliothèque de Vulgarisation*, vol. LI, 1935), and in an even earlier article I compared the band of Luperci who wield the *februa*, with the mythical group of Gandharva (*Le problème des Centaures, Annales du Musée Guimet, Bibliothèque d'Etudes*, vol. XLI, 1929). At that time, however, I did not draw sufficient attention to the relationships between the Luperci and the flamines in Rome and between the Gandharva and the brahmans in India. Such an investigation is very instructive. Let us first review some of the facts.

Rex-Flamen, Rāj-Brahman

Even as late as the Republican era, the hierarchy of Roman priests was headed by the *rex sacrorum* and the *flamen dialis*, who were not two independent priests but a priestly couple. This also must have been so in the very early state when the Roman rex was at the height of his power; and the legend of how the office of flamen dialis was established does in fact make it clear that this personage is merely a subdivision of the rex! Numa created it so that "the sacred functions of the royal office might not be neglected" during those absences that wars inevitably imposed upon the rex (Livy I, 20). Previously, the rex, including Numa himself, had concentrated in his own person what was later split between the essence of the *regnum* and that of the *flamonium* (cf. Plutarch's theory in number 113 of his *Roman Questions*). Religious practice confirms this legend: the insignia of the flamen dialis and of his wife the flaminica were the insignia of the rex and the regina. The dialis had a royal cloak, a royal throne, and, on set days, passed through the city in a royal vehicle (*Lex Iulia Municipalis*, 62; cf. Livy, I, 20). His wife sacrificed *in regia*, "in the royal house," and he himself appeared ritually with the rex (*Pontifices ab rege petunt et flamine lanas, quis veterum lingua februa nomen erat.* "From king and flamen the priests seek the thongs, which in the old tongue were called *februa*," Ovid, *Fastes*, II, 21-22). Lastly, the rex and the major flamines were all "inaugurated"; and it was the same social organ, the very ancient *comitia curiata*, that inaugurated them.

In India, in the very earliest times, *rāj* (or *rājan*) and *brahman* existed in a true symbiosis in which the latter protected the former against the magico-religious risks inherent in the exercise of the royal function, while the former maintained the latter in a place equal to or above his own. As Indian society, at a very early stage, solidified the Indo-European tripartite division of social estates into "castes," and brahman and rāj became the eponyms of the two highest castes (*brāhmaṇa*, *rājanya*), so the same interdependence is to be observed, broadened in its scope but just as clear in its mechanism, between the *brāhmaṇa* (member of the priestly caste) and the *rājanya* (or *kṣatriya*, member of the warrior caste). This interdependence, a commonplace in the literature of every epoch, is defined in numerous texts. Sometimes (Manu, IX, 327) the third caste, that of the *vaiśya*, the herdsmen-cultivators, "to whom the Lord of Creatures gave charge solely of cattle" is contrasted with the *brāhmaṇa* and *rājan* "bloc," who are in charge of "all creatures." Sometimes (*ibid.*, 322), in an internal analysis of that bloc, we read that the *rājanya* cannot prosper without the *brāhmaṇa* nor the *brāhmaṇa* "increase" without the *rājanya*; but that by uniting or "overlapping" (*sampṛktam*), the essences of the two castes (neuter *brahman* and neuter *kṣatra*) will "increase" both in this world and in the other world. As early as the Vedic texts, which precede the classical caste system, the reduced solidarity of rāj and brahman is stated clearly (*Ṛg Veda*, IV, 50, 8): "He lives prosperous in his abode, to him the earth is prodigal of all its gifts, to him the people [*viśah*, literally, the groups of herdsmen-cultivators; *viś* is the word that produced the derivative *vaiśya*, the name for the people of the third caste, and, alongside the neuter terms *brahman* and *kṣatra*, denotes the essence of that third caste] are obedient of their own accord, that *rājan* in whose house the brahman walks in first place (*yasmin brahmā rājani pūrvaḥ eti*)."

I attempted to establish what the structure of this interdependence was during those very early times, why the rāj wished to maintain within his household a personage to whom he yielded precedence. Evidence from ritual and legend led me to believe that this brahman "joined" to the king was originally his substitute in human sacrifices of purification or expiation in which royal blood itself had once flowed.[1] The simulated human sacrifices still performed in the purificatory ceremony of the Argei in Rome, and the major role played in that ceremony by the flaminica, with her display of mourning and grief,[2] seemed to me to confirm this interpretation of the Indian evidence. However, all that is distant prehistory. By the time Indian society becomes observable, the brahman is already far from that probable starting point. It is not with his sacrificial death that he serves the rājan but with his life, each moment of which is devoted to the administration and "readjustment" of magic forces. In historical times the same is true in Rome, where the flamen dialis, *assiduus sacerdos, quotidie feriatus*, constantly robed and solely *ad sacrificandum constitutus*, assures the magic health of the *respublica*, heir of the *regnum*.

The Statutes of the Flamen Dialis and the Brahman

It also seemed of interest to compare the lists of positive and negative obligations that constrained these two "magic instruments," these two living palladiums. Let me briefly recapitulate their similarities (apart from penal immunity, and apart from the singular gravity of brahmanicide and the crime inherent in *flamini manus iniicere*).

The flamen dialis cannot be made to swear on oath (Plutarch, *Roman Questions*, 44; Aulus Gellius, X, 15; Livy, XXXI, 50); and the brahman can never – any more than the king, the ascetic, the madman or the criminal – be cited as a witness (Code of Vishnu, VIII, 2).

The flamen dialis must not so much as look upon armed troops (Aulus Gellius, X, 15); the brahman must suspend his sacred knowledge – that is, his reason for living – whenever he hears the hiss of arrows, or is in the midst of an army, and so on (Manu, IV, 113, 121...).

The flamen dialis, apart from being forbidden any journey outside Rome, must neither mount a horse (Aulus Gellius, X, 15; Plutarch, *Roman Questions*, 40) nor, even for the purpose of sacrifice, touch one (Pliny, *Natural History*, XXVIII, 146); the brahman must not study on horseback nor, it seems, sit on any animal or in any vehicle (Manu, IV, 120).

The flamen dialis must not approach a funeral pyre (Aulus Gellius, X, 15); the brahman must avoid the smoke from a funeral pyre and cease his sacred studies in any village where a funeral procession is passing (Manu, IV, 69, 108).

The flamen dialis must avoid drunkenness and abstain from touching fermented substances (Aulus Gellius, X, 15; Plutarch, *Roman Questions*, 109, 112); the brahman must not consume alcoholic drinks (Manu, XI, 94, 96, 97; cf. *Śatapatha Brāhmaṇa*, XII, 9, 1, 1).

The flamen dialis must not anoint himself with oil in open air (Plutarch, *Roman Questions,* 40); the brahman "after having rubbed his head [with oil] must not touch any part of his body with oil" (Manu, IV, 83; cf. 84, 85, 111, and V, 25).

The flamen dialis is forbidden to touch raw meat (Aulus Gellius, X, 15; Plutarch, *Roman Questions,* 110); the brahman must not eat any meat that has not first been offered in sacrifice (Manu, IV, 213; cf. 112: V, 7, 27, 31, 33, 36, 48, 53), and he must never accept anything from the owner of a slaughterhouse (*ibid.*, IV, 84-86), of a distillery, of an oil press or of a house of prostitution.

The flamen dialis may not touch or even name a dog (Plutarch, *Roman Questions,* 111); the brahman may not read the Vedas when he hears a dog bark (Manu, IV, 115) nor eat food that has touched a dog, or has come from people who breed dogs (*ibid.*, 208, 216).

The flamen dialis may not, even at night, completely divest himself of his priestly insignia (Appian, *Civil War,* I, 65; Plutarch, *Roman Questions,* 40) and his wife must retire only by way of an enclosed staircase so that her undergarments might never be seen (Aulus Gellius, X, 15); the brahman must never strip completely naked, and he must never see his wife naked (Manu, IV, 45, 144, 43).

The brāhmaṇī, the wife of the brahman, and the flaminica, wife of the flamen dialis, are no less important, in a religious context, than their husbands. In Rome and India alike, it is the couple, the husband *with* the wife, who performs the expected magic function. This is natural, given that their role is essentially to provide stable prosperity and regular fecundity. Theoretically, in both cases, the strictest decorum and fidelity are required. One of the most solemn of the eight modes of marriage in India is termed "brahman marriage" (*brāhmaṇavivāha*); similarly, the flamen and flaminica must be married in accordance with the most religious of such rituals, the *confarreatio* – a ritual, moreover, that they must themselves preside over (see my *Flamen-Brahman*, pp. 60-63).[3]

The flamen dialis is "taken" or "seized" (*captus*) by the State and removed from his father's jurisdiction. The high pontiff, having seized him, presents him to the god and, with the help of the augurs, requests the god's assent (*in-auguratio*). The Indian legend of Śunaḥśepa, which legally establishes the superiority of brahmans over all other men, likewise depicts the young brahman as being bought by the king from his father and then presented for the god's assent (*Flamen-Brahman*, pp. 45-46).

The list of coincidences could be extended even further, but I shall add only one here. The color of the brahman is white (a constant doctrine in accordance with the Indian theory of the *varnāḥ* or "castes" - more literally, "colors"), and he consequently wears white clothes (Manu, IV, 35). Similarly, the distinctive headwear of the flamen dialis is termed *albogalerus*, and Ovid, upon seeing a procession of the *flamen quirinalis* on its way to the feast of the Robigalia (*Fastes*, IV, 905ff.), describes it in two words: *alba pompa*. This coincidence, like several others, extends to the Celts, among whom the Druids wore white during their priestly duties both in Gaul (Pliny, *Natural History*, XVI, 49; XXIV, 103) and in Ireland (Arbois de Jubainville, *La Civilisation des Celtes*, 1899, p. 112*n*.). That white is the color of both brahman and flamen dialis becomes even more significant when we recall that red is the color of the Indian *rājanya* and also the mark of the Roman rex (Plutarch, *Romulus*, 26) as well as the Irish *rî*. (A Pahlavi text [translated by M. Widengren as *Hochgottglaube im alten Iran*, Uppsala, 1938, p. 247] also extends this social symbolism of white and red to Iran.)[4]

The Sanskrit *brahman*, to judge by the Avestic *barəsman* (the bundle of sacred rods held by the officiating priest) must derive, with reverse guna, from **bhelgh-men-* or **bholgh-men-*. The Latin *flamen* must derive from a neighboring form, **bhlagh-smen-*, which, along with forms having the radical *-el-* or *-ol-*, presents the same shift (still obscure, but doubtless capable of interpretation by means of Benveniste's theories on root structure) as that evidenced, within Latin itself, by *flavus* as opposed to *fel*, *lana* as opposed to *vellus*, and *pravus* as opposed to the pejorative *per-* (*perfidus*, etc.).

Februus, Fecundation and Gandharva

Once at the end of every year, on the *dies februatus* in the middle of the month of *februarius*, the great purification called *februatio* took place. It was celebrated with the aid of various accessories termed (in the neuter plural) *februa* and ensured by divinities about whom the Roman historians no longer knew a great deal: Iuno Februa (Februata, or Febru(a)lis) and Februus. The rites were performed by a brotherhood that played no other role in Roman life but which, on that one day alone, threw aside all restraint. Two groups of Luperci, made up of young men from the equestrian order, ran through the city naked except for leather belts striking females with thongs of goatskin in order to make them fertile. We do not know what the concluding rites of this violent scenario were, although we do know that goats were sacrificed before the race through the city, that the bloodied sacrificial knife was wiped on the foreheads of the bands' two young leaders, and that they were expected to laugh at that point. We also know that the Luperci sacrificed a dog.[5]

There are "historical" accounts that claim to explain the origin of these rites. The Luperci, they say, were imitating the *pastoralis iuventus*, the young men who had gathered around Romulus and Remus. Their name, like that of the Lupercalia, was an allusion to the two brothers' foster mother, the she-wolf, and to their childhood in the wilderness, during which their hearts became hardened and the seeds of their harsh future were sown. Moreover, the race through the city was said to commemorate a particular episode in the brothers' lives: one day, when Romulus, Remus and their companions were lying naked, lazily watching their meat roast, they were warned that strangers were stealing their cattle. The two bands threw themselves into action without taking the time to dress. The group led by Remus had the good fortune to rescue the cattle and to return to the encampment first, where they tore the barely cooked meat from the spits. "The victor alone," Remus declared, "has the right to eat of it." (It is reasonable to hazard that this singular feature had some corresponding moment in the rites that has not come down to us.) Finally, we are told that the flagellation of female passers-by referred to another, more scabrous incident in the Romulus story: having kidnapped the Sabine women for his men, the young leader discovered, to his annoyance, that they were sterile. He consulted an oracle, which replied: "Let a he-goat penetrate the Roman women!" An augur then rendered a somewhat more decorous interpretation of this robust injunction: the women were struck with goatskin thongs, and they conceived.

The type of feral and brutal brotherhood featured in this episode of Rome's religious life has already been illuminated by ethnography. It is one of those "men-only societies" – societies characterized by disguises, initiations and extraordinary magical powers – such as can be found among almost all so-called semi-civilized peoples – societies that merit, at least in part, the description "secret," and which do not surface in public religious life except to oppose (and then overwhelmingly) the normal mechanism of that religion.

The early Indo-European world could not have failed to possess this essential organ of collective life, an organ of which the Germanic world, in ancient times and even into the Middle Ages, certainly provides more than mere vestiges, and of which the winter and end-of-winter "maskers" of modern Europe are, in part, a bastardization. It seemed to me that the *februatio* of the Lupercalia must have been the Roman adaptation of such scenarios, and I supported this opinion with comparative arguments drawn principally from the Indo-Iranian world.

In India, where the earliest literature is entirely sacerdotal in nature, one can nevertheless discern the existence of at least one such brotherhood. Though transformed into a band of supernatural beings, somewhat divine and somewhat demonic in character, called Gandharva, it can be recognized by one typical characteristic: *men may join it by initiation.* Moreover, just as the Luperci and the Lupercalis are mythically underwritten by the childhood, feral upbringing and early adventures of Romulus and Remus, so, too, the Gandharva educate heroes (Ayus, Arjuna and so on). In the *Ṛg Veda* the outward appearance of the (singular masculine) Gandharva is left vague, but in later writings the (masculine plural) Gandharva are beings with horses' heads and men's torsos who live in a special world of their own. As early as the hymns, moreover, they already stand in a precise relationship to horses and to the harnessing of chariots, those of the Sun and those of men alike, and they retain this feature throughout the epic literature. They are drinkers who steal the soma and other intoxicating drinks, who carry off women and nymphs *(Apsaras)*, and who cheerfully live up to the ribald adjectives applied to them. Some ritual texts also claim that every woman's first mate, before her husband, is a Gandharva. The initiation scene to which I just alluded is found in the touching legend of the two lovers Purūravas and Urvaśī. The earthly king Purūravas is united with the nymph Urvaśī, who lives with him on the condition – as in the Psyche and Mélusine stories – that he never show himself naked to her. The Gandharva, impatient to recover Urvaśī come by night and steal the two lambs that she loves like children. Without taking time to dress, the king rushes out in pursuit, whereupon the Gandharva light up the sky with a flash of lightning. Urvaśī sees her lover's naked body, and she vanishes. Purūravas laments, so pitiably that in the end Urvaśī allows him to find her. He meets her on the last night of the year *(saṃvatsaratamīṃ ratrīm)*, and the next day the Gandharva grant him a wish. Upon Urvaśī's advice he chooses "to become one of the Gandharva." The Gandharva then teach him a particular form of igneous sacrifice (the accessories of which are made from the wood of the *aśvattha* tree, which contains the word *aśva*, "horse," in its name), which allows him to "become one of the Gandharva." Furthermore, while among the Gandharva, Urvaśī bears him a son named Ayus (literally, "vitality").

Finally, is there any need to point to the numerous analogies, both in form and behavior, that link the Gandharva to the Greek centaurs? The centaurs have horses' bodies and male human torsos; they are prodigius runners; they live in a land of their own, as wild as one can imagine; they are great drinkers, sensual, ravishers of women (especially of young brides), and also include among their number at least some artists, scholars, and *educators of heroes*. In particular, Peleus, the beneficiary and victim, like Purūravas, of a "melusinian" marriage, delivers his son, the young Achilles, to the centaur Chiron, who nurtures him for several years with the right amount of bone marrow and wisdom.

Phonetics and Sociology

Several of these resemblances were recognized very early on, and, as the two names sounded well together, the "Kentauros-Gandharva" equation was one of the earliest proposed. But the question was badly defined: time was wasted on reducing these strong personalities to naturalistic symbols. What is actually involved in both cases is the transposition into myth of an ancient society with animal disguises and initiations, a society that "educates heroes," a society linked with horses, and one that certainly had a monopoly on the Indo-European "masters of horses" just as the society of the Luperci still belonged to the *iuniores* of the equestrian order.[6]

The similarities among these three groupings – Gandharva, Kentauroi, and Luperci armed with *februa* – are quite clear, even though they appear at different levels of representation. Luperci, in a ritual practiced at the end of every year, centaurs, in fabulous narrative, and Gandharva, in legends in which we glimpse a ritual (year-end) reality, all display the same fundamental features. Like the flamen and the brahman they either form or recall a religious instrument, one that is impossible to define in today's languages with a single word, but that sociologists, alerted by those secret societies found among the majority of half-civilized peoples, are able to classify without difficulty. We are therefore justified in regarding the identity of the three names *Gandharva, Februo-, Kentauro-* – give or take a few articulatory nuances – as a probability. From the phonetic point of view alone, it is true, they can be explained in several divergent ways, but a convergent explanation is also possible: *Gandharva* by Indo-European **G^{u}hondh-erwo-*, *Februo-* by IE **G^{u}hedh-rwo-* (for the ending cf. *-ruus* from **-ṛwo* in *patruus*), *Kentauro-* by IE **Kent-ṛwo-*. The differences between the first two can be explained by quite normal shifts (different vocalic stages, presence and absence of "nasal infix"). As for the third, its unvoiced occlusives *(k-t-)*, contrasting with the voiced aspirate occlusives *(g^{u}h-dh-)* of the other two, insert it into a set of doublets collated by Vendryes (*Mémoires de la Société de Linguistique*, XVIII, 1913, p. 310; *Revue Celtique*, XL, 1923, p. 436), and this consonantal shift, appearing precisely in roots that indicate a swift or expressive movement of hand or foot ("seize," "run," "recoil"), as well as in names of animals ("he-goat") and parts of the body ("head"), would be appropriate on more than one count in the names of beast-men, Indo-European maskers, swift runners, and great ravishers.

I have already replied on several occasions to another objection; but I want to repeat that reply, since it concerns an important methodological argument that I still hope will bring all linguists over to my position.[7] Some writers have argued, against this etymology of *februo-*, that initial *f* and internal *b* in Latin can derive not only from **g^{u}h-* and **-dh-* but also from many other Indo-European phonemes or phoneme groups (four for Latin *f-* : IE **bh-*, **dh-*, **ghw-*, **dhw-*;

two for Latin *-b-*: IE **-b-*, **-bh-*), so that **gᵘhedhr̥wo-* is only one of *fifteen* equally imaginable and credible Indo-European prototypes for the Latin *februo-*. Agreed. But such indeterminacy is possible only if one refuses to take meaning into account. A totally similar theoretical indeterminacy does not prevent linguists from recognizing in the Latin *feber, fiber,* for "beaver," the equivalent of the Gallic *bebro* (French *bièvre*), the Cornish *befer,* the Irish *beabhar,* the Lithuanian *bêbrus,* and the Old Slavonic *bobrŭ,* all meaning "beaver." In other words, they are quite happy to select from the large number of possible prototypes for *feber* the one that enables them to link it with the Celtic and Balto-Slavonic words, to wit, **bhebhro-*, cf. **bhebhru-*. In short, the identity of meanings seems to them here, quite rightly, a sufficient ground for decision. Yet the same is true in the case of the Latin *februo-*, with the one difference that the beaver can be denoted exhaustively by a single word and recognized at a glance, which gives linguists who are not sociologists the reassuring impression of a simple and concrete concept, whereas "brotherhoods of men-animals characterized by initiation, purificatory violence, and periodic fertility rites, and so on" cannot be denoted today without a long description. Yet, for all that, such brotherhoods are clear-cut, more or less constant social groupings among semi-civilized peoples.

As for the formation of the word, it clearly presents some obscurities, which is hardly to be wondered at. Ten years ago Antoine Meillet urged me to see in it the Indo-European root **gᵘhedh-* (Greek *Πόθος*, etc. "to have a passionate desire for." In any case, the suffix would have to be complex. It is better to give up all attempts to analyze a word that probably no longer had any clear formation in the various Indo-European regions.

Chapter II

Celeritas and Gravitas

Luperci and Flamines, Gandharva and Brahmans

If the analyses of the preceding chapter are correct, then in both the Roman and the Indian cases – that of Luperci as opposed to flamines and that of Gandharva as opposed to brahmans – we are dealing with two sets of representations that are not merely different but antithetically opposed to one another.[1]

They are opposed first, and most obviously, in the duration of their "social presence." The brahmans, like the flamines and the priestly hierarchy they head, represent that permanent and constantly public religion within which – except on one lone day of the year – the whole life of society and all its members is set. The Luperci, as with the group of men the Gandharva seem to represent in mythic transposition, constitute precisely that one exception. Both these groups belong to a religion that is neither public nor accessible, except during that one fleeting appearance (in Rome on February 15, in Vedic India on "the last night of the year"). It is a religion that in fact does not exist, in its later Roman form, other than in that one irruption, and that could not, in any case, in any earlier forms be anything other than constantly secret, apart from on the day of the Lupercalia.

They are opposed also in their innermost purpose: flamines and brahmans are the guardians of sacred order, Luperci and Gandharva are the agents of a no less sacred disorder. Of the two religions they represent, one is static, regulated, calm; the other is dynamic, free, violent. And it is precisely because of its inherently explosive nature that the latter cannot remain dominant for anything more than a very brief period of time, the time it takes to purify and also to revivify, to "recreate" the former in a single tumultuous irruption of energy. The activity of the flamines and brahmans, in contrast, is coextensive with social life by its nature; they are the guarantors, and to some degree the embodiment, of the rules, of those sets of religious and, in a general sense, social prescriptions which are symbolized in Iran by one of Mazdaism's great archangels and which elsewhere led in two different directions – in India to an unlimited proliferation of ritualistic knowledge and philosophy, and in Rome to a new art, that of human law.

They are opposed, lastly, in their mythic resonance. Even the Romans, unimaginative as they were, recognized in the Luperci something of "the other world." One of the gods of the Lupercalia, Februus, is vaguely related to a god of the infernal regions, or else his name is regarded as another name for the feral Faunus. Moreover, the "guarantor legends," the stories about the birth, childhood and early companions of Romulus and Remus, are fabulous: the first Luperci grew up apart from human societies; before founding Rome they represented, for the Albani or the "city dwellers," the brigands of "the bush," given to sudden appearances, raids, incursions. There is nothing of this in the tradition accounting for the origin of the flamines: it was a considered act, a calculated social innovation in which there was no room for the slightest hint of the supernatural. The Indians, albeit always inclined to add mythic overtones to any reality, did not add a divine component to the brahman until quite late; and even if, as I believe, the myth of Brahmā creating the world by self-immolation is in fact only a transposition onto a cosmic scale of an early and savage scenario of human sacrifice, it is incontestable that the personification of Brahmā is philosophic above all, and that the neuter "brahman" contributed as much, if not more, to it as the masculine "brahman." The Gandharva, in contrast, even before the earliest documented evidence, were consigned wholly to the realm of the imagination. They are not even known to us other than in their mythic transposition; they are not *equites* – a human social class – but half-human, half-equine monsters; as part god, part demon, they inhabit a world of their own, "the world of the Gandharva," and so on.

By the late Roman Republic, the Lupercalia – as we know from the attempts undertaken by the early emperors to restore them – had declined in importance. Even so, evidence of that importance still persisted in the ritual itself: the consuls joined in the run as Luperci; and it was during the Lupercalia, during the race itself (undoubtedly with reference to a tradition that has not come down to us in any other form), that Julius Caesar and Mark Antony planned to restore the monarchy. Lastly, the fact that Rome's justificatory legends are all situated within the exploits of its founder, and indeed constitute their essential elements, is sufficient indication that the festival, at least before its decay, carried equal weight, both as to solemnity and efficacity, with the religion that prevailed the rest of the year, and also that it related to sovereignty.

In India, all the early documentary evidence we have concerns the "brahman religion." Since a "Gandharva religion" could never be expressed in these writings, neither the singular nor the plural "Gandharva" are mentioned, except within their mythical transposition. It is only later, in Buddhist works or in a less occlusive state of Brahmanism, that the word "gandharva" came to be used to denote a category of humans, beings who certainly retained some element of the Gandharva of prehistory but who were by now chastened, impoverished, neutralized: these later "gandharva" are "musicians." As a whole, moreover, the early hymns and rituals are not hostile to either singular or plural Gandharva. They regard them not as demons but as genies, who have their own life and customs and with whom it is best to maintain good relations. The fundamental opposition between brahman and Gandharva surfaces on occasion, however; for example, in the lines of the *Ṛg Veda* (VIII, 66, 5) in which Indra is celebrated because "he has smitten the (singular) Gandharva into the bottomless darkness," and has done so "on behalf of the brahman so that they may prosper" *(abhi gandharvam atṛnad abudhneṣnu rajassu ā Indro brahmabhyah id vṛdhe).*

Antithetical Rules of Conduct

Both in Rome and in India, moreover, we have a simple and sure way of testing whether or not this antithesis actually exists. The brahman and the flamen dialis, as we saw earlier, have certain features in common, and are constrained, in particular, by a certain number of identical or analogous obligations and interdicts. If I am correct, it is likely that Gandharva and Luperci will be characterized by features, by freedoms or obligations, diametrically opposed to the pair – brahman and flamen dialis. This is easy to establish.

In Rome, for example, all Luperci belong to the *equites* or knightly order (see the conclusive evidence collected by Wissowa, *Religion und Kultus der Römer,* 2nd ed., 1912, p. 561, n. 3 and 4); whereas the flamen dialis is forbidden either to ride or touch a horse. As *equites,* each of the Luperci wears a ring, and it is with a ring on his finger, holding the *februa* in his right hand, that the Lupercus of the *Ara Pacis* is represented beside the flamines (Domaszewski, *Abhandl. z. röm. Religion,* 1909, p. 92n. etc.); whereas the flamen dialis is forbidden to wear a ring unless it is open and hollow (Aulus Gellius, X, 15).

The Luperci sacrifice a dog (Plutarch, *Roman Questions*, 68); the Lupercalia begin with the sacrifice of a goat, whose blood is then smeared on the foreheads of the two leading Luperci, while its hide is cut into strips and used by the Luperci as whips (Plutarch, *Romulus*, 21, and so on). In contrast, the flamen dialis must neither touch nor name either dog or goat (Plutarch, *Roman Questions*, 111, where, in the case of the dog, Plutarch himself stresses the contrast between the two behaviors).

The Luperci run through the city naked, in imitation of their prototypes, the companions of Romulus and Remus, who in hot pursuit of cattle thieves did not stop to clothe themselves; whereas the flamen dialis has a complicated style of dress that must never be wholly removed.

The mythic prototypes of the Luperci, Remus and his companions, devour meat still hissing from the flames (*verubus stridentia detrahit exta*, Ovid, *Fastes*, II, 373); whereas the flamen dialis must never touch raw meat (Aulus Gellius, X, 15; Plutarch, *Roman Questions*, 110).

One of the two bands of Luperci bears the name "Fabii" (Ovid, *Fastes*, II, 378-379) or "Fabiani" (common form); whereas the flamen dialis must neither touch nor name the bean, *faba*.

The main activity of the Luperci as they run through the city is to whip the women they encounter, and possibly men as well (Plutarch, *Romulus*, 21, and so on); whereas a condemned man who, being taken away for a flogging, throws himself at the feet of the flamen dialis cannot be whipped that day (Aulus Gellius, X, 15).

With their skin whips the Luperci bring fertility to all the women they encounter, without selection or restriction; their prototypes, Romulus and his companions once carried off the Sabine women who were later also collectively whipped and anonymously made fertile at the first Lupercalia. In contrast, the flamen dialis and the flaminica are a model couple, married in accordance with the strictest of all such rituals; they typify the essence of conjugal solidarity and fidelity.

In India, the contrast between the characteristic features of the Gandharva and the interdicts or obligations imposed on the brahmans is no less clear-cut.

The Gandharva are drinkers, whereas the brahmans abstain from drinking. The Gandharva are half-horse, and also tend horses; whereas the brahmans, as we have seen, must cease all religious activity while on horseback. The brahman must never strip himself completely naked, whereas the story of Purūravas, in which he "becomes one of the Gandharva," begins with a lamb-stealing episode in which the Gandharva cause Purūravas to chase after them without taking the time to clothe himself. The Gandharva are so free in their pursuit of sensual pleasure that the summary union of a man and woman is termed "a Gandharva marriage" (as we noted, several texts even say that the Gandharva possesses every woman before her husband does, a claim that we should probably take literally and apply to gandharva-men in masks). In contrast, the brahman must be austere, reserved and passionless; the form of marriage termed "brahman marriage" is one of the most solemn and ritualistic of all.

One particular opposition merits special attention, and even if the Romans, who were not much inclined to either philosophy or art, offer no equivalent, the legends of the centaur Chiron, at once physician, teacher, astronomer and musician do, proving that this is an essential feature: the brahman devotes his life to sacrifice, meditation, and commentaries on the Vedic hymns; he is concerned neither with the arts, human science, nor anything original or in any way related to inspiration or fancy. Indeed, song, dance and music are specifically forbidden to him (Manu, IV, 64). The Gandharva, in contrast, are specialists in these fields. They are such good musicians that their name was very early (or possibly always) synonymous with "earthly musician" (cf. in the epic literature *gānd-*

harva "music"). Moreover, this characteristic is certainly ancient since in Iran, although the Avesta and the Mazdean texts speak of the _Gandarəva_ (_Gandarep..._) only as a monster killed by a hero engaged in virtuous exploits, Firdausi introduces into his poem a certain Kndrv (i.e., Genderev), who is the steward in charge of the pleasures of the demonic king Dahāk. Further, this Kndrv is required by Dahāk's conqueror, Faridūn, to organize festivities in honor of his succession, in an event that includes a great deal of carousing and music.

The opposition, as well as the symmetry, of the concepts denoted in Indo-European by *_bhelgh-men-_ and *_g_^{u}_he(n)dh-r̥wo-_ is evident even in the grammatical use made of the words involved. In Latin the inanimate _februum_, the name of the "instrument of violent purifications and fertility rites that the Luperci must hold in their hands while performing their duties," stands in the same relation to the animate masculine "Februus," "patron god of the Lupercalia" (and so to the animate masculine Sanskrit "Gandharva") as, in Indo-Iranian, the inanimate Vedic "bráhman" ("sacred formula, incantation, and so on," and, even more precisely, the inanimate Avestic _barəsman_, "sacred bundle held by the officiating priest during sacrifice") do to the animate masculine Sanskrit _brahmán_ (nominative _brahmā_) "sacrificing priest," later "Brahmā," "divine creator of the world by his auto-sacrifice." (We know that the Latin nominative _flamen_ combines an animate value with an inanimate form of the same type as _agmen_, _certāmen_, and so on. The normal animate form would be *_flāmo._)

Certainly, then, we are dealing with antithetical religious concepts and mechanisms. From the standpoint of method, perhaps it would be best at this point to stress that everything first put forward as a result of a direct comparison between brahman and flamen, then between Gandharva and Lupercus, is now seen to be indirectly reinforced by the fact that the Indian brahman-Gandharva antithesis corresponds exactly with the Roman flamen-Lupercus antithesis. If my "horizontal" comparisons had been artificial, then the artifice would have been revealed by at least some degree of discrepancy in the "vertical" relationships. When it comes to abstract reasoning and constructions, regularity and harmony do not provide the slightest presumption of correctness. But we have not been reasoning in the abstract; rather, we have simply drawn up a register of concrete facts. Material of this sort will not long tolerate the imposition of an order not derived from its own nature and history.

The flamen-Lupercus and brahman-Gandharva antitheses share still other aspects and areas of incidence that I shall touch on only briefly.

Celeritas and Gravitas

The Luperci, the Gandharva and the centaurs are all "swift." All of them, ritually or mythically, are runners in important or famous races; and although this characteristic is doubtless closely linked with their nature as *equites* or their semi-equine form (on the importance of the horse in Indo-European societies, see Koppers, *Pferdeopfer und Pferdekult der Indogermanen, Wiener Beitr. z. Kulturgesch. und Linguistik*, IV, 1936, pp. 279-412), it is also in conformity with a more general mystique. Speed (extreme rapidity, sudden appearances and disappearances, lightning raids, etc.) is that behavior, that "rhythm," most suited to the activity of violent, improvisational, creative societies. In contrast, the ordered public religion that holds sway throughout the year, except for that brief period when the masked monsters are unleashed, demands a majestic gait and solemn rhythm. The Romans expressed this in an arresting formula: the bodyguards of Romulus, the first Luperci, are called the *Celeres* (from *celer*, "swift"); and the successor of Romulus, Numa, began his reign with two complementary acts: he dissolved the *Celeres* and organized the triple *flāmonium* (Plutarch, *Numa*, 7). This opposition between the mystique of *celeritas* and the morality of *gravitas* is fundamental, and it takes on its full meaning when one recalls that the dizzying intoxication of speed – among the shamans of Siberia and on our own Grand Prix circuits – is just as much a stimulant, an intoxicant, a means of achieving an illusory transcendence over human limitations, as is alcoholic intoxication, erotic passion or the frenzy stirred by oratory. We know that Mazdaism placed its own particular imprint on this opposition with the notion of the headlong *run* versus the majestic *walk*: all "ahurian" beings, even when they are heroes doing battle or fighters on behalf of good, are always described simply as "going," "coming," "walking" (roots *i-, gam-*); "daêvian" beings alone (demons, monsters, wicked rulers, and so on) "run" (roots *dvar-, dram-*). (See H. Güntert, *Ueber die ahurischen und daêwischen Ausdrücke im Awesta, SB d. Heidelb. Ak d. W., ph.-hist. Klasse*, 1914, 13, sections 14-16, pp. 10-11; cf. Louis H. Gray, *Journ. of the Roy. Asiat. Soc.*, 1927, p. 436).

Iuniores et Seniores

It seems that the Luperci and the flamines were also antithetically differentiated as *iuniores* and *seniores*. There are reasons for thinking that this classification by age, although it plays a restricted role in historical Rome, was much more important in early times (cf. my article "*Jeunesse, Eternité, Aube*" in the *Annales d'histoire économique et social*, July 1938, p. 289ff.). The Luperci are *iuvenes* (*equestris ordinis iuventus*: Valerius Maximus, II, 2); their founders are the two archetypal *iuvenes* surrounded by youthful companions (*Romulus et frater pastoralisque iuventus*), and as I argued in the article just mentioned (pp. 297-298), both the Gandharva and *Kentauroi* societies, at the time when they functioned within human reality, seemed also to have enjoyed a sort of privileged right over "the maximum vitality, over the *akmé* of life" (Sanskrit *ayus*, Greek *αἰών*, IE **ayw-*), in other words, over what constituted the very essence of the Indo-European **yu(w)-en-*, according to the elegant analysis by

E. Benveniste (*Bull. de la Soc. de Ling. de Paris*, XXXVIII, 1937, pp. 103-112). As for the flamines and the brahmans, although they cannot be congenitally assimilated into the *seniores* (since one can be *captus* as flamen dialis at a very early age, and one is born a brahman), their affinity and their "equivalence" to the *seniores* are nevertheless strongly indicated: they need only practice the morality of their station with the required rigor in order to have the rank of *seniores*. On this point I shall draw on two traditions only; but the agreement between them is significant.

We read in Manu, II, 150-155: "The brahman who gives (spiritual) birth and teaches duty, even if he be a child, is according to law the father of a man of years (*bālo 'pi vipro vṛddhasya pitā bhavati dharmataḥ*). Kavi, son of Angiras, while still young (*śiśuh*) taught the sacred knowledge to his paternal uncles (*pitṛn*, literally, "fathers") and addressed them as 'Sons!' *(putrakā iti hovāca*). Angered, they demanded of the gods the reason for this. The gods gathered and answered: 'The boy spoke to you correctly, for the ignorant man is a child, he who gives the sacred knowledge is a father...; it is not because he has white hairs that a man is old (*na tena vṛddho bhavati yenāsya palitaṃ śiraḥ*); he who has read the Scripture, even when young, is classed by the gods as an elder (*yo vai yuvapy adhīyānas taṃ devāḥ sthaviraṃ viduḥ*).'" This well-known legend acquires its full meaning when we take into account the fact that it occurs in support of the definition, given in the preceding sloka (149), of the actual name of the brahman or "spiritual father," and that the name is said there to be *guru*, or "heavy." This means that the brahman carries within him the same physical image as that conjured up by the name for the supreme virtue of the Roman *seniores*, which is *gravitas*.

Now, in Livy, XXVII, 8, we read: "And Publius Licinius, the pontifex maximus, compelled Gaius Valerius Flaccus to be installed as flamen of Jupiter, although he was unwilling.... I should gladly have passed over in silence the reason for installing a flamen perforce, had not his reputation changed from bad to good. Because of his irresponsible and debauched youth, Gaius Flaccus was seized *(captus)* as a flamen by Publius Licinius. As soon as the responsibility of rites and ceremonies took possession of his mind, Gaius reformed his old character so suddenly that no one among all the young men *(iuventute)* of Rome stood higher in the estimation and approval of the leading senators *(primoribus patrum)*, neither within their own families nor among strangers. By the unanimity of this good reputation, he acquired a well-founded self-confidence and claimed that he should be admitted to the senate (*ut in senatum introiret*), a right that had long been denied former flamens because of their unworthiness. After, having entered the Senate House the praetor Publius Licinius led him away, he appealed to the tribunes of the plebeians. The flamen insistently claimed the ancient right of his priesthood, saying it had been granted to that office of flamen along with the *toga praetexta* and the *sella curulis (vetustum ius sacerdotii repetebat, datum id cum toga praetexta et sella curuli et flamonio esse)*. The praetor maintained that right should be based, not on outmoded instances from the annals, but on very recent practice, and that within the memory of their fathers and grandfathers no flamen of Jupiter (flamen dialis) had exercised this right. The tribunes held that obsolescence was due to the indolence of flamens and was justly accounted as their own loss, not a loss to the priestly office. Whereupon, without opposition even from the praetor and with the general approval of the senators and of the plebeians, the tribunes led the flamen into the senate, for everyone agreed that the flamen had proven his point by the uprightness of his life rather than by virtue of his priestly privilege (*magis sanctitate vitae quam sacerdotii iure eam rem flaminem obtinuisse*)." This fine text is interesting in several respects. First, for the psychology of the praetor, that great artisan of Roman law, whom we see here attempting to modernize a rule by the legalization, after a lapse of several generations, of a spontaneous innovation. Second, for the opposition it depicts between the *impetus* of the free *iuvenis* and the *gravitas* of the flamen. Last, because it bears witness to the fact that the flamen dialis, in ancient times, was admitted by right into the assembly of that particular set of *seniores* made up of the *senatores.* This last point provides a curious link with the Indian tradition and doctrine dealt with earlier.

Creation and Conservation

Flamines and Luperci, brahmans and Gandharva, all share equally in the task of securing the life and fecundity of society. But here again it is instructive to note the contrast between the behaviors involved. Not only in the area, dealt with earlier, of their conduct toward women – on one side, individual, sacrosanct marriage and fidelity; on the other, kidnap, sensuality and anonymous fertilization – but in the very purpose and principle of that behavior. One group ensures a continuous fecundity against interruption and accident; the other makes good an accident and reestablishes an interrupted fecundity.

If a celibate flamen dialis is inconceivable, if India "centers" the career of every brahman on his role as husband and head of family, if the flaminica and the *brāhmaṇī* are just as holy and important as their husbands, it is all because the presence and collaboration of this feminine element shows that the principal mechanism of fertility is in a healthy state, that all the female forces of nature are functioning fully and harmoniously. In Rome the evidence is particularly clear: should the flaminica die, the flamen dialis immediately becomes unfit to perform his functions, and he resigns. The flamen-couple must have children, and those children must also take part in the couple's sacred activity. If the couple do not have children of their own, then they take as flaminii the children of another family, both of whose parents are still alive. All these rules signify the potential or actual continuity of the vital flow. The many taboos that oblige the flamen to keep away from funeral pyres, from dead animals, from barren trees, anything that has succumbed to natural decay or failure, are perhaps intended less to protect him from taint than to express the limitations of his activities: he is powerless against that which has already occurred. In other words, although, he can prolong life and fecundity through his sacrifices, he cannot restore them.

That miracle – of restoring fecundity – is on the contrary the great feat performed by the men-animals. In Rome their whipping race commemorated the act by which their legendary prototypes ended the sterility of the women carried off by the first king, Romulus. In India they restored the lost virility of the first sovereign, Varuṇa, with herbs known only to them. The mystique underlying these traditions is not difficult to reconstitute: it is that of the emasculation of Varuṇa's Greek counterpart, Uranos, at once an unbridled, excessive procreator and a tyrannical, intolerable sovereign, who lost his genitals and sovereignty simultaneously. The sterility that strikes the Sabine women because Romulus had the audacity to abduct them from their husbands, the sterility that threatens Rome and the empire at the very moment of its formation, has the same meaning – with a more precise reference to the hubris of Uranos – as the "devigoration" that strikes Varuṇa at the very moment of his consecration as *saṃrāj* or universal sovereign (cf. my *Ouranos-Varuṇa*, ch. IV and V). It is no chance coincidence that the restorer of Varuṇa's virility is the (singular) Gandharva (*Atharva Veda*, IV, 4) and that the restorers of the Sabine women's fertility are the Luperci with their *fabrua*. Excess – the very cause of the accident – also provides the remedy. It is precisely because they are "excessive" that the Gandharva and the Luperci are able to create; whereas the flamines and the brahmans, because they are merely "correct," can only maintain.

I have referred at several points to the fact that the Luperci were instituted by Romulus and that the flamines were instituted (or organized) by Numa. I am thus led to inquire whether the antithesis that underlies the two priesthoods, these two organs of magico-religious sovereignty, is not to be found in the history of the two first kings, the two sovereign-archetypes of Roman history.

It is also noteworthy that the Gandharva are called "Varuṇa's people" (*Satapatha Brāhmaṇa*, XIV, 4, 3, 7), and in the paragraphs above that deal with the sterility of the women stolen by Romulus and the impotence of Varuṇa (the former cured by the Luperci, the latter by the Gandharva), we can discover an important clue: in terms of his function, does not Romulus embody an archetype of the "terrible" sovereign in Roman history, comparable to the archetypal figure I explored in an earlier work with reference to Varuṇa and the Uranos of the Greek cosmogonies? Further, just as Roman history sets Numa, patron of the major flamines, beside Romulus, leader of the Luperci, so India juxtaposes, closely and antithetically associated in a way that ensures their collaboration, Varuṇa and Mitra: Varuṇa, who has the Gandharva as his people, and Mitra, who is normally associated with the brahman. New perspectives now begin to open up, perspectives that become clearer still when we take into account the "favorite" gods of both Romulus and Numa. In the case of Romulus they are the "terrible" variations of Jupiter; in the case of Numa, Fides. And Fides is the personification of contractual correctness, as is, beside Varuṇa, the omnipotent magician, the Indo-Iranian *Mitra.

Chapter III

Romulus and Numa

The Singular Relationship of Romulus and Numa

Romulus and Numa are the two "fathers" of the Roman state. In Plutarch Romulus is compared to Theseus, Numa to Lycurgus. Although these comparisons are instructive, they conceal one important difference: Lycurgus did not succeed Theseus, since each ruled his own city; Numa, on the other hand, did succeed Romulus. Thus, in this instance they both worked on the same material yet modeled it differently.

This relation greatly perplexed the annalists. For even if they knew, generally speaking, that Romulus founded the city in a material sense, whereas Numa was responsible only for its institutions, they still wondered why Rome had to wait (if only during Romulus's lifetime) for the creation of the religious or social institutions that ancient thought and experience found to be so primary and germinal to the existence of the city. Take, for example, the worship of Vesta with its College of Vestals. The logic of the system required that its founder should be Numa, since the Vestals are part of the same whole as, say, the flamines, and since they form an essential part of the "establishment" religion, of the most unchallenged domain of *gravitas*. Tradition did in effect lay the honor for all that – the priestesses, the form of worship, the sanctuary – at the feet of Numa. But how, on the other hand, could one accept that Rome had been forced, before Numa, to do without the sacred fire, the entire community's source of energy and solidarity, especially when it was so simple and so much in conformity with all known customs to think that Romulus had brought with him, to his "colony," a spark of the sacred fire from the "mother city," Alba Longa? This was a surprising intellectual dilemma, and some authors, whose reasons are clearly put forth by Dionysius of Halicarnassus (*Roman Antiquities*, II, 75; cf. Plutarch, *Romulus*, 22), did not hesitate to make Romulus the founder of the national hearth even at the risk of dismantling Numa's achievements. Others went further. To them it seemed impossible that Numa should have been the creator even of the *flamonium*; so he simply "completed" or "reorganized" it.

The annalists were also placed in a delicate situation by the fact that Numa's work emended that of Romulus. And emended it in such a way that in many instances it actually replaced it with its opposite. In short, Numa's work implicitly condemned that of Romulus. Yet Romulus could not be in the wrong. And certainly he was not in the wrong, for the Roman state owed him not only its birth but also certain examples of conduct that, despite being contrary to those of Numa, were nonetheless useful, accepted and sacred. How then to prove that Numa was wise, without stigmatizing as faults, crimes or follies the salutary violence of Romulus? The Roman historians extricated themselves from this dilemma with some skill. They managed to displace the conflict into the realm of abstract notions such as "peace" and "war," so that praise and blame could be avoided (cf. the excellent summary by Livy at the conclusion of Numa's reign [I. 21]: *duo deinceps reges, alius alia via, ille bello, hic pace, civitatem auxerune... tum valida, tum temperata et belli et pacis artibus erat civitas.* "Thus two kings in succession, by different methods, the one by war, the other by peace, aggrandized the state... the state was both strong and well versed in the arts of war and peace"). But, more often, they skirted around these issues carefully, and they accepted the fact that, as in the life of societies and individuals, the most conflicting practices can be harmoniously reconciled – provided that one does not constantly insist on abstract principles.

So much for the ancient writers. As for the moderns, they have subjected the legends of Romulus and Numa to the most detailed scrutiny, and the results of the various critiques are certainly interesting. The literary history of Romulus has been carefully traced, and in the case of Numa it has been established (sometimes with certainty, sometimes not), from which now-lost works Livy or Dionysius or Plutarch borrowed such-and-such a feature. But one must not exaggerate either the scope or the conclusions of this research. It is only very rarely, and generally without absolute certainty, that we are able to transcend literary history and put our finger on the true origin of any detail. To say that Livy took this or that from Valerius Antias does not mean that we know whether Valerius Antias invented it or borrowed it, with a greater or lesser degree of distortion, either from a particular author, genteel tradition or mere rumor. So, when we have taken the whole thing apart and ascertained (as much as possible) the approximate legitimacy of each element, there still remains another line of inquiry and another "point of view," which together might constitute the essence of the matter: What are the *main trends* within the whole? What are the *lines of force* running through the ideological *field* within which all the details are placed? But let me not search for too modern an image simply to formulate the old and futile problem of not being able to tell "the forest from the trees." And since the trees in this case have found so many observers already, surely a comparatist may be allowed to concentrate his attention on the forest. Certainly it is indisputable that the lives, the works and the very figures of Numa and Romulus, even allowing for some inconclusiveness of detail, were conceived of throughout the entire tradition as strictly antithetical. And it is clear, too, that this antithesis coincides, in many of its manifestations, with the ritual and conceptual antithesis analyzed in the previous chapter.

Numa as Antithesis of Romulus

Romulus made himself king. He and his brother left Alba because they were possessed by the *regni cupido*, the *avitum malum* (the "ambition of sovereignty," the "hereditary evil") (Livy, I, 6) and could not accept not being rulers there (Plutarch, *Romulus*, 9). Romulus tricked the augurs at Remus's expense, then killed him or had him killed in order to become sole ruler (Plutarch, *Romulus*, 9-10). Later, at the insistence of the Roman people, who were unanimous in their reverence for his wisdom (Plutarch, *Numa*, 5-6), Numa consented to become king, but with repugnance and regret at leaving a quiet life in order "to serve."

Romulus is the typical *iuvenis* and *junior*. His career as an adventurer begins with his birth. With the *iuvenes* (later given the title *Celeres*) (Plutarch, *Romulus*, 26), his constant companions in both peace and war (Livy, I, 15), he governs in such a way as to incur the hostility of the *patres*, of the *senatores* (Plutarch, *Romulus*, 26-28). He would disappear suddenly, either by miracle or as a result of murder, at "the height of his powers," and then appear immediately afterward to one of his friends "fair and stately to the eye as never before" (28-29). On the other hand, Numa is already forty (and his life hitherto had been one of long seclusion) when he was offered the *regnum* (Plutarch, *Numa*, 5) on the recommendation of the *senatores* (*ibid.*, 3), after an interregnum during which Rome was governed by the *patres-senatores* (*ibid.*, 2). His first act is to dissolve the *Celeres*, his second to organize the triple *flamonium* (*ibid.*, 7), or rather to create it (Livy, I, 20). He lives to be extremely old, past his ninetieth year, and slowly dies of old age, of a "languishing sickness" (*ibid.*, 21). In legend, he came to be the "white" king (Virgil, *Aeneid*, VI,

809); at his obsequies the *senatores* carry the funeral bed on their shoulders (Livy, I, 22); and he remained the standard by which *gravitas* was measured (Claudian, *Against Rufinus*, I, 114: *sit licet ille Numa gravior...*).

Everything Romulus does is warlike; even his posthumous advice to the Romans is to cultivate the art of war ("*rem militarem colant*") (Livy, I, 16). Numa makes it his task to break the Romans of their warlike habits (Plutarch, *Numa*, 8); peace remains unbroken throughout his reign (*ibid.*, 19, 20). He even offers a friendly alliance to the Fidenates when they raid his lands and on that occasion institutes the *fetiales*, priests whose concern it is to guarantee respect for the forms that prevent or limit violence (Dionysius of Halicarnassus, *Roman Antiquities*, II, 72; cf. Plutarch, *Numa*, 12).

Romulus kills his brother; he is at least suspected of the death of his colleague Tatius (Plutarch, *Romulus*, 23). In the "asylum" that was later to become Rome, he indiscriminately welcomes and protects all fugitives: murderers, defaulting debtors, runaway slaves (*ibid.*, 9). He has the Sabine women carried off (*ibid.*, 14); his violence engenders the no-less violent hostility of the senators who, perhaps, tear him to pieces (*ibid.*, 27). Numa is wholly without passions, even those held in esteem by barbarians, such as violence and ambition (Plutarch, *Numa*, 3). He hesitates before accepting the kingship because, knowing that Romulus was suspected of his colleague's death, he does not want to risk being suspected, in turn, of having killed his predecessor (*ibid.*, 5). His wisdom is contagious: under his rule sedition is unknown, there are no conspiracies, and men live exempt from disturbances and corruption (*ibid.*, 20). His greatest concern is justice, and the reason he wishes to dissuade the Romans from war is because war engenders injustice (Plutarch, *Parallel between Lycurgus and Numa*, 2).

Romulus practices trickery in religion (Plutarch, *Romulus*, 9) and "invents" the god Consus only to use his feast day as an ambush (*ibid.*,

14). Numa's entire life is founded on religion, on religious uprightness; he institutes not only new forms of worship but also the correct outward forms of meditation and piety (Plutarch, *Numa*, 14). He establishes almost all the priestly colleges (*ibid.*, 7-10) and takes upon himself the task of teaching the priests (*ibid.*, 22).

Women and family have almost no place in Romulus's life; he has the Sabine women abducted only to perpetuate the Roman race. Although he himself marries one of them (according to some versions only, for example, Plutarch, *Romulus*, 14), he does not, properly speaking, found a *gens*: either he has no children or else his children have "no future," since they play no part either in person or through their descendants in Roman history. Moreover, it is to Aeneas, not to Romulus, that the emperors were to trace back their title to power. Admittedly he treats the Sabine women honorably when they have procured the consent of their husbands and fathers (*ibid.*, 20), but that does not prevent him, once they proved sterile, from indiscriminately whipping them to make them fertile (Ovid, *Fastes*, II, 425-452, and elsewhere). In truth his whole career, from start to finish, is that of a bachelor, and he establishes a harshly unfair regime of marital repudiation, much to the detriment of married women (Plutarch, *Romulus*, 22). Numa is hardly to be thought of, any more than a flamen dialis, without his wife, Tatia, with whom, until her death thirteen years later, he forms a model couple (Plutarch, *Numa*, 3). Tatia, or a second and no less legitimate wife, gives Numa a daughter, who will become the mother of Ancus, another pious king of Rome, and according to other sources, four sons who are the ancestors of "Rome's most illustrious families" (*ibid.*).

Plutarch has Numa say the following in explaining his reasons for refusing the *regnum*, and in so doing he unwittingly gives a very accurate account of the situation (*Numa*, 5): "Men laud Romulus as a child of the gods and tell how he was nurtured in an incredible way and fed in a miraculous manner when he was still an infant. But I am mortal by birth, and I was nourished and trained by men whom you know...." This opposition is indeed an important one, and is similar to the antithesis remarked upon earlier between the Luperci and the flamines and, in India, between Gandharva and brahmans: Luperci and Gandharva, bearers of mysteries, are usually from another world, and are mere transients in this world to which brahmans and flamines rightfully belong. The Romans portrayed Romulus, like the Luperci, in as supernatural a fashion as their rational imaginations allowed, whereas Numa was seen as part of the complete, reassuring humanity of the priesthoods he instituted.[1] Moreover, the Romulus-Numa opposition, under all the headings just listed, coincides even down to its underlying principle with the Luperci-flamines opposition: on one side, the tumult, passion and imperialism of an unbridled *iunior*; on the other, the serenity, correctness and moderation of a priestly *senior*.[2] This general "intention" of the two legends is clearly more important than the scattering of individual, inevitably varying details through which it is expressed.

Moreover, this opposition of the two founding kings is also strikingly expressed in the contrast between their "favorite" gods.

Romulus and Jupiter, Numa and Fides

During his entire life, Romulus founded only two cults. Moreover, they were not cults of Mars, as one might have expected had he been nothing more than a self-made warrior-chief. Rather, they were cults of Jupiter, as is natural to a born sovereign; however, these cults represent two very precise specifications of Jupiter: Jupiter Feretrius and Jupiter Stator. The two legends are linked with the wars that followed the rape of the Sabine women.

Romulus slew Acro, king of Caenina, with his own hand, in single combat, and thus won the battle. In thanks, or else in fulfillment of a vow, he raised a temple to Jupiter Feretrius (the first Roman temple, according to Livy) and there offered King Acro's arms to the gods – the first *spolia opima*. This is a royal cult, a cult in which Jupiter is very much the same Jupiter as that of the old hierarchized triad Jupiter-Mars-Quirinus; in other words, the god of the head of state, the god of the *regnum* (cf. Livy, III, 39, who says that *rex* is a name that it is *fas* to apply to Jupiter). Indeed, Roman tradition was to record only two other cases of *spolia opima*, and these offerings were made, in decreasing importance of the triad, to Mars (Cossus, after victory over one of the Veientian kings "in 428 B.C.") and then to Quirinus (Marcellus, after victory over a Gallic chieftain in 222 B.C.: Servius, *Commentary on the Aeneid*, VI, 859).[3] But this Jupiter, Jupiter Feretrius, is god of the rex only in one of the aspects of the rex himself; a rex fighting in single combat in the name of his whole people, and a rex victorious. The words that Livy attributes to Romulus are significant in this respect: *Iupiter Feretri, haec tibi victor Romulus rex regia arma fero*...: "Jupiter Feretrius, I, king, Romulus, upon my victory, present to thee these royal arms..." (I, 10; cf. Plutarch, *Romulus*, 16).

Jupiter Stator saved Rome at a moment of grave danger. As a result of the Tarpeian treachery, the Sabines were already in possession of the citadel and on the verge of defeating the Roman army on the plain between the Palatine and the Capitol. The Romans were panic-stricken, and Romulus invoked Jupiter: *Deme terrorem Romanis, fugamque faedam siste!* "Dispel the terror of the Romans, and stay their shameful flight!" Courage returned instantly to the Roman forces, who halted their flight, attacked and drove the Sabines back "as far as the place where the House of the King (*regia*) and the temple of Vesta now stand." In thanks, Romulus dedicated a temple to the god of their salvation on the very spot where the marvel took place (Plutarch, *Romulus*, 18; Livy, I, 12). And marvel this certainly was: upon invocation of the *rex*, Jupiter instantly and invisibly intervened, took the whole situation into his hands, and reversed the course of the battle. We shall soon have the means to explore the significance of this event; but for now the Roman data are clear enough.

Thus these two specifications of Jupiter coincide in this respect: they both show Jupiter as the divine protector of the *regnum*, but specifically in battles, in victories. And the second victory is the result of a supreme being, a sovereign conjuring trick, a piece of public sleight-of-hand against which no human or superhuman power is of any avail, and this overturns the expected, the "correct" order of events. Jupiter Feretrius, Jupiter Stator, both are Jupiter as king, violent and victorious. And Jupiter Stator is in addition a great magician.[4]

In contrast, all the authors stress Numa's particular devotion to the god Fides. Dionysius of Halicarnassus writes (*Roman Antiquities*, II, 75), "There is no higher or more sacred sentiment than faith (*πίστις*), either in the affairs of the state or in relations between individuals. Being persuaded of this truth, Numa, the first of mankind in this, founded a shrine dedicated to *Fides Publica* (*ἱερὸν Πίστεως δημοσίας*) and instituted, in her honor, sacrifices as official as those to other divinities." Plutarch (*Numa*, 16) also says that Numa was the first to build a temple to Fides and that he taught the Romans their greatest oath, the oath of Fides. Livy (I, 21) tells us that Numa established an annual sacrifice to Fides, and that for this event the flamines – clearly the three major flamines – drawn in a single chariot and working together (in other words, symbolizing the cohesion of the social functions represented in early Roman times by the names of Jupiter, Mars and Quirinus), performed the ceremonies with their right hands entirely swathed. This last feature, Livy adds, in agreement with known tradition, signified "that *fides* must be constantly protected, and that anything in which it resides, including the right hand, is sacred" (*significantes fidem tutandam, sedemque eius etiam in dextris sacratam esse*).

Fides and Śraddhā

What the author means here by *fides* is clear. In private as in public life, within the city as well as in relations with outsiders, *fides* is a respect for commitments, a respect for justice (which means that Numa's devotion to Fides is linked to one of the general characteristics by which he was defined earlier in contrast with Romulus). This meaning is generally accepted in all the different contexts where *fides* is discussed: we have just noted Livy's comment about the right hand, and Plutarch makes a significant comparison between the cult of Fides and that of Terminus, which Numa founded, he says, with a similar intention, that of "protecting peace and convicting injustice." "It was he [Numa]," Plutarch tells us, "who set the boundaries of the city's territory, for Romulus was unwilling to acknowledge, by measuring his own, how much he had taken away from others. He knew that a boundary, if observed, fetters lawless power; and if not observed, leads to injustice" (*Numa*, 16; cf. *Roman Questions*, 15). Among the reasons he offers for the establishment of the cult of Fides Publica, Dionysius of Halicarnassus (II, 75) says that Numa had observed that, among contracts in general (*Τῶν συμβολαίων*), those that have been drawn up publicly and before witnesses are protected by the *honor* of the two parties (*ἡ Τῶν συνόντων αἰδώς*) and are rarely violated; whereas those, much more numerous, that have been sealed without witnesses have no other guarantee than the *good faith* of the contractors (*Τὴν Τῶν συμβαλόντων πίστιν*). From this Numa concluded that he should give good faith his greatest support and so be made a god of *fides*. Finally, we know that the institution of the *fetiales*, which is generally attributed to Numa (and otherwise to Ancus, his grandson and emulator), was founded to preserve peace through the strict observance of agreements and, when that was not possible, to lend to the declaration of war and to the conclusion of treaties a regulated and ritualistic character. In short, Numa's *fides* is the foundation of Rome's supreme creation, its law.

At the same time, however, it is something very different. Modern writers have often marveled at the way Roman law, from the very outset, appears to have been distinct from religion, the way in which it is constituted, from the first, as a work of reason and reflection, as well as of observation and experiment; in fact, it was truly scientific in its technique. And they are right to marvel. Yet, however precocious this Roman "miracle" might have been – less prestigious perhaps, less multiform, but no less honorable than the Greek miracle – it is impossible to conceive that, in the very earliest times, the future law of the Romans could have been any more separable from their forms of worship and their theology than it is in most semi-civilized societies observable today. The notions on which the early jurists worked, and on which their modern commentators have reflected, can only have been stripped gradually of the magico-religious elements that, in the beginning, constituted the largest, the most certain, the clearest part of their content. This is the case with the substantive *fides*. And on this point comparative linguistics has long since assembled the necessary data.

Antoine Meillet (*Mémoires de la Société de Linguistique de Paris*, XXII, 1922, pp. 213-214 and p. 215ff.) has shown that the word *fides* (root **bheidh-*: Greek *πείθω*, and so on) serves as a verbal substantive to *credo*; in other words, that it must have replaced an early **crede* (from **kred-dhe-*, with stem legitimately in *-e-*), by which it seems to have been influenced early on, since it too, without any possible direct justification, has an *-e-* stem. *Fides* and *credo*, in other words, share the same domain: not merely that of law but also that of religion, and additionally, between those two, that of ethics. So when Christianity gave the substantive noun "faith" and the verb "believe" the overtones they still have today, it was at the very least rediscovering and revivifying very ancient usages.

Indeed, among the religious expressions shared by the Indo-Iranian, Italic, and Celtic worlds, one of the most striking is that which subsists in the Sanskrit *śrad dadhāmi, śraddhā-*, and so on; in the Avestic *zrazdā-*, and so on; in the Latin *credo*; in the Old Irish *cretim*, and in the Old Welsh *credaf*. It is also one of the most intensively studied both analytically and comparatively. The Vedic concept of *śraddhā* has been explored by Sylvain Lévi in *La doctrine du sacrifice dans les Brahmanas*, 1898, p. 108ff., and its Iranian forms explained by Antoine Meillet in *Mém. de la Soc. de Linguist.*, XVIII, 1913, p. 60ff. The undoubtedly related Celtic words have been dealt with by M. Vendryes in *Revue Celtique*, XLIV, 1927, p. 90ff. While M. Ernout, in *Mélanges Sylvain Lévi*, 1911, p. 85ff. (eliminating the link with Romance forms of "heart") and A. Meillet, in *Mém. de la Soc. de Ling.*, XXII, 1922, (*op. cit.*) have provided the theory of the Latin forms and of the family as a whole.

Magic and Religion

Sylvain Lévi's work is of particular importance. Using a great number of texts, he has shown that the word *śraddhā*, at first understood rather too hastily as "faith" in the Christian sense of the word, or at least as "trust," in fact denotes something slightly different in the consciousness of the ritual-minded Indians. Correctly understood, it means at most something akin to the trust that a good workman has in his tools and technique. It would be more correct, Lévi says, to place *śraddhā* on the level of magic than on that of religion, and to understand it as denoting the state of mind of a sacrificer who knows how to perform his office correctly, and who also knows that his sacrifice, if performed in accordance with the rules, must produce its effect. Needless to say, such an interpretation is to be viewed within a more general system that, as the ritualistic literature suggests or states in many places, is based on the dogma of the omnipotence of sacrifice. Within this system, sacrifice with its code and its attendants, ultimately emerges, above and beyond the gods, as the sole motive force in this or any other world.

Lévi's *La Doctrine du Sacrifice dans les Brahmanas* is an admirable book and would still be so if written today – despite the plethora of indexes and catalogues we now have as opposed to the research required in 1896-1897. At that time, the new sociology, in search of clear-cut notions, was striving not only to distinguish between magic and religion but also to define a series of precise levels for each religious phenomenon such as, in this case, sacrifice. The pupil always collaborates with the master, and this was undoubtedly the case with Marcel Mauss and Sylvain Lévi, as the lectures from which Lévi's book emerged were intended to help the young sociologist in his work. And I don't think that I, in my turn, am being disloyal to Marcel Mauss if I observe that he speaks not only much more frequently of "magico-religious" facts than of magical facts, on the one hand, and of religious ones on the other, but also that one of his principal concerns is to show the complexity of each phenomenon, and the tendency of each to defy definition and to exist simultaneously on many different levels. Such, certainly is the natural consequence of the article he published in 1899 ("Essai sur la nature et la fonction sociale du sacrifice," *Année Sociologique*, II) and in 1904 ("Origine des pouvoirs magiques dans les sociétés australiennes," 13th *Annuaire de l'Ecole des Hautes Etudes, Sciences Religieuses*, pp. 1-55). In the human sciences one can, with some precision, define points of view or the directions one's exploration of particular material is to take; but, excluding exceptional cases, the material itself evades simple classification and disconcerts the observer with its metamorphoses. Perhaps we should keep this in mind when evaluating the account that Sylvain Lévi drew up in his day.

Not that the "doctrine of sacrifice" in the *brāhmaṇa* is in any way different from that which Lévi derived from them: the primacy, the automatism, the blind infallibility of sacrifice that he alleges are indeed established in formulas too clear to dispute. But we ought not to draw conclusions from a very specialized literature, the work of the technicians of sacrifice, and apply them to the whole of contemporary life. And one must not be too quick, even within that literature itself, to regard as a survival, as a mark of "primitive mentality," the more magical than religious form taken on by the relations between man and the mystic forces he sets in motion.

The religion of the Vedic era is rich in individualized gods, most inherited from the Indo-Iranian community, some from the Indo-European community. Possessed of precise personal powers, sometimes the nucleus of proliferating mythological cycles, these gods are not "literary ornaments." They are, both for one another and for man, intelligent, strong, passionate, active partners. And this is hard to reconcile with an absolute automatism of gestures and formulas. We must at least retain as a possibility the hypothesis that the guild of officiants systematically increased the constraining power of sacrifice. Far from being a survival, such a system could have been developed at the expense of the older Indo-Iranian gods' erstwhile freedom. So, the notion of *śraddhā*, we doubtless should accept that it was already animated by movements of "piety," "devotion," "faith," even at a time when the ritualists were reducing it to nothing more than an almost purely technical attitude within an almost impersonal form of worship. A religious concept is rarely to be defined by a *point*, but more often by an *interval*, by a zone in which variable movements, unstable relationships, are established between two poles. Where does incantation end? Where does prayer begin?

Whatever the nuance of meaning we fasten upon for the Indian *śraddhā*, however, at whatever level we place this "trust," it is certain that the prehistoric Latin **credes* was capable of expressing analogous values. Numa, in short, is not only the specialized devotee of Fides as "good faith" among men, as a guarantee of human contracts; he also practices a sacrificial *fides*, the same as the *śraddhā*, and one that similarly allows the observer a margin of interpretation between the certainty of the magician and the faith of the priest.

The Sacrifices of Manu and of Numa

At this point, we should note the remarkable agreement between the Indian and Roman traditions concerning Numa and Manu, the two fabled legislators and sacrificers: Numa is the true hero of *fides*, just as Manu is the hero of *śraddhā*.

The Indian traditions relating to Manu's *śraddhā* are well known. Sylvain Lévi, in his *Doctrine du Sacrifice* (pp. 115-121), has given an excellent account of them; indeed, this one sentence sums them up well: "Manu has a mania for sacrifice just as the saints of Buddhism have a mania for devotion." The most famous of the stories depicts Manu, enslaved as he is to *śraddhā*, yielding up everything of value he possesses to the two "Asura brahmans," to the demonic sacrificers Tṛṣta and Varūtri. To demand something from him all they need do is say the words, *Mano yajvā vai śraddhā-devo'si* ("Manu, you are a sacrificer, your god is *śraddhā*"). His jars, the sound of which alone could annihilate the Asura; then his bull, whose bellowing replaced the sound of the jars; and, in the end, even his wife, the Manavī, whose speech had acquired that murderous gift – Manu hands them all over, without a moment's hesitation, to be destroyed, sacrificed by the priests who demand them with those words. When Indra, in his turn, wishing at least to save the Manavī, presents himself to Manu in the form of a brahman and announces, using the same formula, that he wishes to make a sacrifice of the two "Asura brahmans," Manu hands them over without any difficulty and, in one variant (*Kāthaka Brāhmaṇa*, II, 30, 1), the two brahmans are actually immolated: Indra beheads them with the water of the sacrifice, and from their blood spring two plants that dry up in the rain. And the god utters the climactic words which in fact justify Manu's conduct: *yatkāma etām ālabdhaḥ sa te kāmaḥ samṛdhyatām* ("the desire you had in taking your wife to sacrifice her, let that desire be granted you") (*Maitrāyaṇī Saṃhitā*, IV, 8, 1; with many parallel texts).

As for Numa, Plutarch (*Numa*, 15; there is also an allusion to this behavior of Numa's in Plutarch's short treatise *On the Fortune of the Romans*) summarizes one legend, no doubt residual from a more abundant tradition relating to the king's piety, in which this Roman is truly *śraddhādevaḥ*: "It is said that he had hung his hopes so exclusively upon the divine that, one day when someone came to tell him that the enemy was drawing near, he laughed and said: 'And I do sacrifice.'" (*Αὐτὸν δὲ τὸν Νουμᾶν οὕτω φασὶν εἰς τὸ θεῖον ἀνηρτῆσθαι ταῖς ἐλπίσιν, ὥστε καὶ προσαγγελίας αυτῷ ποτε γενομένης ὡς ἐπέρχονται πολέμιοι, μειδιάσαι καὶ εἰπεῖν εγὼ δὲ θύω.*) The feeling indicated in that strong expression, *εἰς τὸ θεῖον ἀνηρτῆσθαι ταῖς ἐλπίσιν* (with the neuter *τὸ θεῖον*), and the behavior dictated by this primacy accorded to the act of *θύειν*, would provide an excellent definition of "the doctrine of sacrifice in the *Brāhmaṇa*": Manu would have acted in exactly the same way.

And the Roman tradition might, in its turn, shed light on Indian custom. If Numa's "faith" operates in this way, in a double domain, one almost mystic, the other wholly legal, it is because in Rome acts of worship and sacrifice are, first and foremost, acts of trade, an execution of contracts of exchange between man and divinity. Their automatic nature – which inspires Numa with his confidence – is less magical than juridical. The acts performed have the constraining force of a pact, at least that implicit kind of pact explored by Marcel Mauss in his *The Gift: Forms and Function of Exchange in Archaic Societies* (pp. 6-16; originally published as "Essai sur le don, forme archaïque de l'échange," *Année Sociologique, Nouv. série*, I, 1925, pp. 128-134, 140-152) and which is so well expressed in the traditional formula, *do ut des*: "I give that you may give." And in fact this notion of a divine "trade" is no less essential to the Indian theory of sacrifice (Marcel Mauss has drawn attention to the importance of the formula *dadāmi te, dehi me*, "I give to you, give to me!"). We frequently encounter scenes in which a god evaluates the greater or lesser worth of a proposed offering, or compares the values of two possible victims, and so on. In one famous story, Varuṇa agrees that the young brahman Śunaḥśepa shall take the place of the king's son as the sacrificial victim, "because a brahman is more than a *kṣatriya*." Even the legend summarized above, in which Manu is on the brink of slaying his wife, ends in haggling, with one odd difference: it is Manu who wishes to maintain the assessed initial value, and the god who imposes the "discount." But Manu, deprived of his victim by the merciful intervention of the god, does not intend that his rights be infringed: "Finish my sacrifice," he says to Indra, "let my sacrifice not be set at nought!" And the god generously indemnifies him, in a way: "The desire you had in taking your wife for your victim, let that desire be granted you; *but let that woman be!*" (Sylvain Lévi, *op. cit.*, p. 119).

How can this fail to bring to mind the famous scene in which the pious, ultra-correct Numa bargains with Jupiter to obtain immunity from his thunderbolts, without having to make a human sacrifice – even though, in this case, the roles run more true to form? Here it is the god (a sovereign god, it is true, not a military god, as is Indra) who is exacting, and the king who plays the "bazaar trader," as they would say in the East; who, in other words, argues and barters, who uses his wiles without actually cheating, and yet manages to cheat anyway. At first, Jupiter demands "heads." "Of onions" Numa quickly accedes; "No, of men," the god insists. "I'll give you hair as well, then," the king sidesteps. "No, I want living beings," Jupiter says. "Then I'll throw in some small fish!" Numan concludes. Disarmed, the terrible sovereign of heaven agrees, and immunity from his thunderbolts was obtained from then on at very little cost (Plutarch, *Numa*, 15; Ovid, *Fastes*, V, 339ff.).

Numa's religious "faith" and Manu's *śraddhā* thus share the same domain, rest on the same assurance, are susceptible to the same kinds of transactions. Both combine with the interests of the sacrificer or, rather, reconcile his interests, openly and honestly, with those of the god. The important, the irreplaceable thing for the man is to have a true will to sacrifice, and to sacrifice punctiliously whatever has been decided on beforehand by common accord. However, the quantity and quality of the sacrificial material is an affair for negotiation between the parties.

* * *

It is now time to introduce other elements. All I wished to establish is that, like Romulus and Numa, the two gods peculiar to them, Jupiter Stator (or Feretrius) and Fides stand in an antithetical opposition (whether juridical or religious), to one another. The gods, like the kings, stand opposed as the "Terrible" and the "Ordered," the "Violent" and the "Correct," the "Magician" and the "Jurist," the Lupercus and the flamen. They also stand opposed like Varuṇa and Mitra, with whom there is an even more exact correspondence with the Roman couple – with a masculine form of Fides – Jupiter and Dius Fidius.

Chapter IV

Jupiter and Fides

The Dialectical Nature of Indian Social Hierarchy

The Indians' social hierarchy, like the system of ideas that sustains it, is linear in appearance only. In reality it is a sequence, rather Hegelian in character, in which a thesis summons an antithesis then combines with it in a synthesis that becomes in turn a further thesis, thus providing fresh material enabling the process to continue. For example, *brāhmaṇa*, *kṣatriya* and *vaiśya* (priest, warrior and herdsman-cultivator) are not to be numbered "one, two, three." The *brāhmaṇa* is defined at the outset in opposition to the *kṣatriya*; then the two are reconciled and collaborate in a new notion, that of "power" (*ubhe vīrye*, "the two forces," is the eloquent dual expression in some texts), which is then immediately defined in opposition to *vaiśya* (e.g., Manu, IX, 327), an opposition itself resolved by a synthesis into the *dvija*, "the twice-born," which is then confronted by the appearance of the *śūdra*.

Perhaps it will be possible to pursue the exploration of this classification of the world further at a later stage. I mention it here only to observe it at its source or, rather, at its apparent source, since even the "first echelon" is itself already a synthesis. Perhaps it would be more accurate, at least for very early times (before the rising fortune that expanded the term *brāhmaṇa* to cover an entire caste), to begin with the *rāj-brahman* couple. Yet even in this historical situation we are able to observe, at a time when brahmanic imperialism is at its height, that the elements and formulation of that synthesis remain perceptible if we consider not the brahmans themselves, but the gods who stand behind them, the gods who govern from on high the great business of the brahmans on earth, which is sacrifice, and who also happen to be the sovereign gods, the cosmic projection of earthly sovereignty: Mitra and Varuṇa.

The coupling is an extremely ancient one. These two gods appear as a couple and in that order, heading the list of Aryan gods called upon to guarantee a Hittite-Mitanian (Hurrite) treaty in the 14th century B.C. (*mi-id-ra-aš-šil u-ru-wa-na-aš-ši-el*: Forrer, *Zeitsch. d. deutsch. morg. Gesell.*, 76, N.F., I, 1922, p. 250ff.).[1] There is also a fairly frequent Avestic formula, Mithra-Ahura, which is generally accepted to be an inheritance from the Indo-Iranian past (see Benveniste-Renou, *Vṛtra* and *Vrthagna*, 1934, p. 46, and J. Duchesne-Guillemin, *Ahura-Mithra*, in *Mélanges F. Cumont*, 1936, II, p. 683ff.). This associates Mithra with an Ahura who is not yet the Ahura Mazdāh of historical times, but who is linked to the Asura-type figure of the Vedic hymns, Varuṇa. In the *Ṛg Veda*, as in the *Atharva Veda*, Mitra is inseparable from Varuṇa; and, with one exception, all the *Ṛg Veda* hymns dedicated to Mitra are also dedicated to Varuṇa. Moreover, their language makes the couple's interdependence startlingly plain, since it couples the two divinities in various ways by using dual formations: *Mitrā* is "Mitra and Varuṇa," as is, less elliptically, the reduplicated dual form, *Mitrā-Varuṇā* (with single or dual inflection: *Mitrābhyām Varuṇābhyām* or *Mitrā-Varuṇābhyām*), or the simple dual, with two stresses or one, *Mitrá-Váruṇā*, *Mitrá-varuṇā* (cf. Gauthiot, *Du nombre duel*, Festschrift V. Thomsen, 1912, p. 128ff.).

And, again, the same holds true for this initial couple as for the later couples *Brāhmaṇa-kṣatriya*, *ubhe vīrye-vaiśya* and *dvija-sūdra*: viewed in relation to the rest of the universe, to the other gods (Indra, say), Mitra and Varuṇa form a unit, seem to occupy the same domain (sovereignty), and are, to some extent, synonymous. This collaboration is made possible, however, only by a congenital opposition: Varuṇa is also to be defined as the contrary of Mitra. The authors of the *Brāhmaṇa* were fully aware of this fundamental fact, and we have only to follow them. We also have only to follow Bergaigne, since on this point, as on so many others, his account (*Religion Védique*, 3 vols., Paris, 1878-1883) is still the most useful. If we cannot now maintain his definitions without some amendments, it is only because sociology has progressed, and because certain notions that seemed simple to him have since been revealed as fairly complex; as, for example, that of "friend."

Mitra: Contract and Friendship

By interpreting Mitra as "friend" (and a section of the Indian tradition does so) and by linking Varuṇa to the root *var-* ("to cover, to envelop, to bind") and also to *Vṛtra* (the "bad" or "wicked" *Vṛtra*), Bergaigne was led to formulate the opposition of the two gods as being that of "the terrible" and "the friend," while both, as he happily expresses it, are "sovereigns."

Varuṇa is assuredly "the terrible"; as a result of his magic, of his *māyā* as an *asura*, thanks to which, omnipresent as he is, he has the power of immediate prehension and action everywhere and over everything, and thanks to which he also creates and modifies forms and makes the "laws of nature" as well as their "exceptions." In my own analysis, in which I compare him with the no less terrible, tyrannical and unbridled Uranos, I had many opportunities to illustrate this characteristic of the god. In particular, he has an unfortunate affinity with human sacrifice, both ritually and mythically.

As for Mitra, the word "friend" is clearly insufficient. Yet it is less so today than it appeared in 1907, when Antoine Meillet, in a classic article, put forward his definition of "the Indo-Iranian god Mitra" as the "contract" personified (*Journal Asiatique*, 10th series, vol. X, pp. 143-159). Those few pages are a milestone in the history of our field, since for the first time linguistics and sociology worked together with assurance. But since 1907 the theory of the contract has progressed in its turn with the result that the notions of legal contract and emotional friendship, which seemed scarcely reconcilable to Meillet, now appear as no more than two reductions, two divergent and more clearly defined meanings, both fairly recent, derived and now detached from an earlier "complex" that in fact, has left its vestiges still very much alive not only in India and Iran but even in our own civilizations, as is evidenced by such proverbs as "gifts foster friendship."

Meillet's interpretation was disputed by mythologists faithful to the naturalism of Max Müller, and also by philologists with mistaken notions as to the limits of their jurisdiction. Nonetheless, it is unavoidable as far as Iran is concerned, as a reading of the *Yast* of *Mithra* with an open mind will make clear. As for India, it would be a waste of time attempting to dispute the fact that *mitra* in the *Ṛg Veda* appears to be something quite different from "contract," and that the meaning of "friend" is dominant throughout. But the difference is illusory. It exists only insofar as one conceives of friendship as something modern and romantic, and of the contract as something Latin and, as it were, notarial. One has only to recall the research undertaken in France and elsewhere in response to the discovery of that very widespread phenomenon now termed, using a noun taken from the American Indians of British Columbia, the *potlatch*; one has only to re-read Davy's *La Foi jurée, étude sociologique du problème du contrat, la formation du lien contractuel* (Paris, 1922), and Mauss's book *The Gift*; whereupon the two semantic poles between which India and Iran seem to have stretched the prehistoric **mitra-* begin to seem much less far apart. It becomes apparent that this word, formed with an instrumental suffix or an agent-suffix on the root **mei-* ("to exchange"), this word to which we find so many others related throughout the Indo-European territory – words with nuances of meaning as diverse as Sanskrit *mayate* ("he exchanges"), Latin *munus* ("gift, service performed, obligation, duty") and *communis*, Old Slavonic *mêna* ("change, exchange, contract") and *mirŭ* ("peace, cosmos"), and so on – this word **mitra-* must have originally denoted the means or the agent of operations of the *potlatch* type – in other words, of "obligatory exchanges of gifts." Evolving from customs in general, and doubtless as a result of contact with very early civilizations which possessed codes, the meaning of the word naturally narrowed to the more precise one of "contract," as occurred in Iran. On the other hand, however, the state the potlatch inevitably creates between its participants, of peace, of order, of collaboration, with alternating rights and duties, is indeed a beginning of "friendship," particularly among the semi-civilized, where a simple absence of relations is already equivalent to hostility: India merely developed this germ of meaning in terms of human feelings, without losing sight of its ancient economic and social origins.

As epigraph to his article on the gift, Mauss quotes several stanzas from the *Hâvamâl*, an Eddic poem that describes, in the form of maxims, some of the important motivating forces underlying early Scandinavian societies. Readers will readily appreciate how close and interdependent the notions of "regularized exchanges" and "friendship" are in this text:

> 39. I have never found a man so generous and so hospitable that he would not receive a present nor a man so liberal with his possessions that to receive in return was displeasing to him....
> 41. Friends should please one another with weapons and garments; everyone knows it for himself, that those who give one

another gifts are friends for longest (*vidhrgefendr erusk lengst vinir*), if things turn out well.
42. One should be a friend to one's friend and give back gift for gift (*vin sînum skal madhr vinr vesa, ok gjalda gjöf vidh gjöf*); one should earn laughter for laughter and trickery for lying.
43. You know it yourself, that if you have a friend in whom you trust, and if you wish a long-standing friendship, you must mingle your soul with his, exchange gifts and visit him often... (*veiztu, ef thû vin âtt thanns thû vel truit, ok vildu of hânum gôtt geta, gedhi skaltu vidh thann blanda ok gjöfum skipta, fara at finna opt*).
46. Gifts given should be like those received....

One ought really to explore in greater depth, throughout the Germanic world, the notions expressed in these lines by the verbs *trûa* ("to trust in, to believe") and *gjalda* ("to pay back, to expiate"). I shall limit myself here, however, to pointing out that the Scandinavian noun for "friend," *vinr* (Swedish *vän*; cf. Old High German *winî*), not only is related to the Irish noun for "family," *fine*, which is defined by precise and varied degrees of interdependent responsibility (hence the Old Irish *an-fine*, for "enemy," is formed as the Old Icelandic *ô-vinr*, which has the same meaning), but is doubtless also related to the first element of Latin, *vin-dex* (formed as *iudex* is on *ius*), which expresses essentially a legal notion, the *vindex* being, in fact, "the bailbond provided by the defendant, who replaces it with his person before the court and declares himself ready to submit to the consequences of the legal process" (Ernout and Meillet, *Dictionnaire étymologique latin*). Thus, to judge from the noun that denotes him, the Swedish "friend" (and we know to what peaks of poetry, what depths of delicacy, friendship can attain in that favored land), the *vän*, emerged over the centuries from an economic complex in which self-interest and personal "investment" played a role still present in early medieval Scandinavia, given the evidence accorded us by the

Hâvamâl, and also, no doubt, from a legal complex in which the "vendetta" must have played an important part, since the related Irish and Latin words place it in the foreground. Similarly, again, Irish *cairde* (literally, "friendship," cf. Latin *carus*, etc.) denotes any treaty concluded between two clans, from a simple armistice to the most far-reaching agreements (see the extensive treatment of this in Thurneysen's commentary on the *False Judgements of Caratnia*, section 17, *Zeitsch. f. celtische Philologie*, XV, 1925, p. 326ff.). *Mutatis mutandis*, the relations between Sanskrit *mitraḥ* ("friend," and also, in post-Vedic, *mitram*, in the neuter, "friend, ally") and Avestic *mithra*, "contract," must be of the same sort.

I shall explore in more detail some of the juridical functions of the Indo-Iranian **Mitra*. Here it is sufficient to have pointed them out. But it should also be noted, immediately that they constitute only one part of Mitra's activity as a whole; and that activity, as the earliest Indian ritualists were still aware, was defined at all points by reference, by opposition, to Varuṇa.

Mitra, Antithesis of Varuṇa[2]

Noting in his *Doctrine du Sacrifice*... (p. 153) a passage from the *Śatapatha Brāhmaṇa* (IV, 1, 4, 1) in which Mitra and Varuṇa are contrasted as intelligence and will, then as decision and act, and also another passage from the same *Brāhmaṇa* (II, 4, 4, 18) in which the contrast between them is likened to that between the waning and the waxing moon, Sylvain Lévi observes: "The disparity between these interpretations proves that they are the product of imagination." Yes, if one sticks to the letter of the texts; no, if one takes into account their spirit. Leaving aside the moon, the other two formulas link up with many others,[3] and this collection of "coupled notions" provides an excellent definition of two different ways of regarding and directing the world. When it is said, for example, that Mitra is the day and Varuṇa the night; that Mitra is the right and Varuṇa the left (in accordance with the view of the right as the *strong* or *just* side); that Mitra takes (in order to reward) "that which has been well sacrificed" and Varuṇa takes (in order to chastise) "that which is badly sacrificed"; that this world is Mitra and the other world Varuṇa; that to Mitra belongs, for example, all that breaks of itself and to Varuṇa that which is cut with an axe; to Mitra the unchurned butter, to Varuṇa the churned butter; to Mitra that which is cooked with steam and to Varuṇa that which is roasted over flame; to Mitra milk, to Varuṇa soma, the intoxicating drink; that Mitra is the essence of the brahmans and Varuṇa the essence of the rājanya or *kṣatriya* – all these twinned expressions define homologous points on the two levels we have learned to recognize through Numa and Romulus. Mitra is the sovereign under his reasoning aspect, luminous, ordered, calm, benevolent, priestly; Varuṇa is the sovereign under his attacking aspect, dark, inspired, violent, terrible, warlike. Some of these expressions have been subjected to much commentary, in particular those that assimilated "this world" to Mitra and "the other world" to Varuṇa, and are easily understood in this context. We have already seen that Numa and Romulus, like the flamen and the Lupercus and the religious systems they institute or express (one perpetual and public, the other fleeting and mysterious), and like the brahman and the Gandharva, too, also stand in opposition to one another as the purely "earthly" does to the "supernatural," as this world does to the other. "Romulus was born of the gods and I am a mere man," Numa says when justifying his hesitation at accepting the *regnum*; and the Gandharva normally live in a mysterious world of their own, beyond the darkness into which, according to one of the Vedic hymns, Indra smote the (singular) Gandharva for the greater good of the brahman. Let us not forget that Varuṇa is said elsewhere to have the Gandharva as his people, and that in his legend the Gandharva intervene at a tragic moment to restore his failed virility with a magic herb, just as the first Luperci, wielding their goatskin whips, put an end to the sterility of the women Romulus had abducted.

Mitra as brahman, Varuṇa as king of the Gandharva: we could hardly have wished for a more suggestive formula.

Jupiter and Dius Fidius

There are reasons for thinking that the "order of the gods" and the "order of the flamines," which in Rome record the ancient Indo-European tripartite division of social functions, is no more linear than the brahmanic hierarchy. In the triad of gods, Jupiter and Mars are homogeneous, but Quirinus is not. Whereas Jupiter and Mars are strongly characterized and autonomous, Quirinus alone poses problems: sometimes seen as akin to Mars (from whom he nevertheless remains essentially distinct), sometimes to Romulus (which draws him rather into the ambit of Jupiter), he appears more as "hero" than "god." Whereas *Iupiter* (**dyeu-*) and *Mars* (*Mauort-*: Sanskrit *Marut-aḥ*, name of the warrior-god Indra's warrior band) have certain or probable Indo-European etymologies, *Quirinus* can be explained only in accordance with an Italic origin (cf. *curia, quirites*); and the same is true of Vofionus, who occupies the place of the Roman Quirinus, after a well-established Jupiter and Mars, in the corresponding triad of the Umbrians.[4] When a triad with feminine preponderance came to replace the older masculine triad, the sovereign Jupiter and Juno, goddess of the *iuniores*, emerged quite clearly as a "couple" in our sense of the word (and not merely in imitation of Zeus and Hera), contrasting with a third term, *Minerva*, the goddess of workers. Lastly, if we consider the three major flamines, the Quirinalis, like his god, cuts a poor figure beside the Dialis and the Martialis, who are moreover linked (to judge by a number of inevitably lacunary indications) by a strict "statute" of similar interdicts. In short, given the uncertainties and dilutions only to be expected from the fact that this double *ordo* had lost almost all interest for the late Republic, it seems that vestiges still remained from a time when the composition of these triads of gods and priests was a matter not of simple enumeration but of deduction by successively constructed couples.

At the summit of the hierarchy there stands one "couple" whose existence is well attested, not only by the fact that the flamen dialis appears, both by his activity and by the legend of his institution, as the rex's double, but by the very complexity of the theological province to which the word *dialis* refers. In historical times, flamen dialis and flamen Iovis were accepted as being equivalent terms. But Festus (in his *De significatione verborum*), when describing the *ordo sacerdotum*, glosses flamen dialis with *universi mundi sacerdos, qui appellatur dium*. And this substantive, *dium*, provides us with an opportune reminder that there survived a divinity alongside Jupiter, certainly a very ancient one, who in the historical era seems no longer to be anything more than an "aspect" of Jupiter: Dius Fidius. And Dius Fidius, moreover, enshrines *fides* within his very name.

Not that it is of any great importance here whether, fundamentally, Dius Fidius was an "aspect" of Jupiter or whether he had once been an autonomous divinity later absorbed by Jupiter, since these are mere historical contingencies or, possibly, a simple question of vocabulary. What does count is the articulation of the divine concepts. And the fact is that Dius Fidius, whether alongside Jupiter or as a mere aspect of Jupiter, certainly stands in opposition to certain other "aspects" of the same god.

Dius Fidius, the Antithesis of Jupiter Summanus

Lightning, when there are no nice distinctions to be made, generally belongs to Jupiter. But when such distinctions become necessary, daytime lightning is called *fulgur dium* and is understood to come from Dius Fidius (alias *Semo Sancus*) or from Jupiter (when his name is understood according to the strict etymological value expressed by the root **deiw-*); nocturnal lightning is termed *fulgur* *submanum* (or *summanum*) and is understood to come from a god who is called either *Iupiter Summanus* or simply *Summanus*, and for whom the question of his relations with Jupiter ("aspect" or "absorption") poses itself in the same terms, and has the same lack of importance, as in the case of Dius Fidius.

Weinstock's article on *Summanus* in the Pauly-Wissowa *Encyclopédie* (1932) sets forth all the documentary evidence very clearly; but its conclusions are distorted, in my view, by unwarranted deduction and also by a mistaken assumption. The unwarranted deduction bears upon the "Etruscan" origin of the god, for which Weinstock, opposing Thulin, finds what he takes to be his proof in Pliny's *Natural History*, II, 138 (*Tuscorum litterae novem deos emittere fulmina existimant, eaque esse undecim generum; Iovem enim trina iaculari. Romani duo tantum ex iis servavere, diurna attribuentes Iovi, nocturna Summano*: "The Tuscan writers hold the view that there are nine gods who send thunderbolts, and that these are of eleven kinds; because Jupiter hurls three varieties only, two of these deities have been retained by the Romans, who attribute thunderbolts in daytime to Jupiter and those in the night to Summanus"). However, we cannot conclude from this text, as Weinstock does, that Summanus was "captured" from the Etruscans by the Romans. The comparison between the two systems is typological, and the word *servavere* no more signifies a borrowing in the case of Summanus than in the case of Jupiter, to whom he stands in opposition. Pliny is simply recording the fact that the Roman system does not coincide with the Etruscan system, which, he presumably regards as the more advanced, the more scientific, the more in conformity with reality, and, also, the older; and that, whereas the Etruscans were able to distinguish as many as eleven different kinds of lightning, the Romans have "retained," which is to say "recognize," only a meager distinction between "day lightning" and "night lightning." As for Weinstock's mistaken assumption, this concerns the logical impossibility he experiences in accepting the traditional explanation of the name Summanus (from *sub* and *mane*) and, consequently, its Latin derivation. The transition from "*morgens*" or "*gegen, um, kurz vor Morgen*" to "*nachts*" seems inconceivable to him. "It would be strange," he writes, "if we were forced to look for the word *mane* ("morning") in the name of a god of the night." But we must always be wary of things that seem, to our modern minds, logically impossible or strange. It so happens that another Indo-European language, Armenian, denotes night – the whole of the night, and without any possibility of dispute – by the periphrasis "until dawn" (*c'ayg*, i.e., *c'* "until," and *ayg*, "dawn")[5] and, in parallel, the day – the whole day, and even in modern speech, from "noon" – by the periphrasis "until evening" (*c'erek*, i.e., *c'* "until," and *erek* "evening"). The use of "Summanus" to denote the nocturnal lightning-hurler is no more astonishing, and there is no reason to suspect its latinity.

Day and Night

Jupiter as Dius Fidius and Jupiter as Summanus, or, at some earlier time, an autonomous, heavenly divinity Dius Fidius and an autonomous, heavenly divinity Summanus, may thus be distinguished as the owner of the day and the owner of the night. We have already seen – and J. Muir's *Original Sanskrit Texts* (V, 1870, p. 58ff.) had already highlighted this before Bergaigne – that such is also the naturalist form taken by the opposition of Mitra and Varuna: "the day is of Mitra, such is the tradition...and also the night is of Varuṇa" (*Maitram vai ahar iti śruteḥ...śrūyāte ca vāruṇī rātrir iti*) Sayana says in his commentary on *Ṛg Veda*, I, 89, 3, borrowing the terms of the *Taittirīya Brāhmaṇa* (I, 7, 10, 1). The *Taittirīya Saṃhitā* (VI, 4, 8) states the same fact in cosmogonic terms: "This world had neither day nor night, it was (in this respect) nondistinguished; the gods said to the couple Mitra-Varuna (note the dual form *mitrāvaruṇau*) 'Make a separation!'...Mitra produced the day, Varuna the night"

(*Mitro'har ajanayad Varuṇo rātrim*). Upon these formal statements by the ritualists, Bergaigne (*Religion védique*, III, p. 117) based his reflections which, because of their lucidity, merit lengthy consideration and which, moreover, ought to be extended to all the antithetical features of these two gods:[6] "I propose to show that the distinction made here was already present in the minds of the Vedic poets, albeit without possessing any absolute nature for them. Mitra and Varuṇa, linked to form a couple, are both of them gods of the day and gods of the night, and Varuṇa, even alone, retains a luminous side. But he also has a dark side, and when compared with Mitra it is indisputably this dark side that stands out in contrast to the predominantly luminous nature of his companion." Bergaigne then justifies this broad statement with a well-ordered list of texts, supported (p. 122n.) by a quotation from a hymn in the magical Veda (*Artharva-Veda*, IX, 3, 18) addressed to the *śālā*, the hut constructed for sacrifice: "Closed by Varuṇa," it says, "be opened by Mitra!"[7]

The relations between Jupiter and Dius Fidius are the same. Taken together, their functions coalesce: the oath belongs to Dius Fidius, but also to Jupiter. Similarly, all lightning belongs to Jupiter, though it would be ridiculous to maintain that the Romans essentially sense the night sky in Jupiter. But the standpoint changes when they consider the autonomy of Dius Fidius: from the Jupiter complex there emerges a "nocturnal" power, a Summanus, which enables Dius to define himself, in conformity with his etymology, as "diurnal."

At the sacrificial stake, Mitra, god of day, receives white victims, whereas Varuṇa, god of night, receives black ones (*Taittirīyra Saṃhitā*, II, 1, 7ff., cf. V, 6, 21; *Maitrāyanī Saṃhitā*, V, 2, 5) – an eminently natural symbolism. And this symbolism is also found in Rome, where, as we know from an inscription (*Corpus inscr. lat.* VI, 1, 574), the Arvales sacrificed *Summano patri verbeces atros*. Weinstock, in the *Encyclopédie* article cited earlier, sees this as proof that Summanus has nothing to do with Jupiter. "Jupiter never receives black victims," he says, "whereas such victims appear regularly in the worship of the chthonian gods." This, it seems to me, is not a valid argument. In the single case in which Jupiter is specifically described as "nocturnal" or *summanus*, in contrast to the "diurnal" Dius Fidius, it is natural that his victims, like those of Varuṇa (in his role as "nocturnal" divinity) should be black. It is of no consequence that he does not receive black victims in any other function. Or, rather, one cannot conclude from that circumstance anything other than a close link between the color black and the god's nocturnal specification.

We may also note in passing that this opposition of Varuṇa and Mitra, of the violent sovereign god and the just sovereign god, as "night sky" and "day sky," seems to occur also in the case of the two Greek figures, Uranos and Zeus. Zeus is, beyond dispute, the sunlit sky. As for Uranos, let us not forget how Hesiod introduces the scene of his castration (*Theogony,* lines 173ff., trans. Richard Lattimore, Univ. of Michigan Press, 1959):

> Thus spoke Kronos and giant Gaia
> rejoiced greatly in her heart
> and took and hid him in a secret ambush
> and put into his hands
> the sickle, edged like teeth
> and told him all her treachery.
> And huge Uranos came on,
> bringing night with him . . . (*ἦλθε δὲ νυχτ᾽ ἐπάγων μέγας Οὐρανός*).

As if that terrible god was not capable of consistency, could not act, could not become accessible, except by night; as if he could not even appear without bringing on the night.

Dius Fidius and Fides

That Dius Fidius was the guarantor of good faith and the recorder of oaths is clear from his name, and, moreover, is attested by much evidence. And the nocturnal Jupiter, to whom he stands in opposition, certainly participates in the magical, disturbing nature of the night. So we have been led back to the opposition – doubtless not merely analogous but in fact identical to this one – of the two "favorite" gods of the grave Numa and the violent Romulus: that of Fides and Jupiter in his terrible aspect (Feretrius or Stator).

Needless to say, in the case of oaths as in that of lightning, Dius Fidius is not in conflict with Jupiter, with "the other Jupiters." We must not forget that these oppositions define complementaries, not incompatibles, and that, viewed in relation to the rest of the world, gods and men alike, this group of divine figures or divine aspects presents a common front. Consequently, although many texts, as well as the expression *me Dius Fidius* and much well-known ritual evidence, prove that the oath is properly the realm of Dius Fidius, the tradition as a whole nonetheless places the oath under the protection of Jupiter or, rather, under that of the deity I would like to term "Jupiter in general." Similarly, in India, even though it is Mitra who carries contractual correctness within his actual name, this does not prevent Varuṇa from occasionally being a god of oaths. It is true that this apparent confusion, in Rome and India alike, might have overlaid an earlier and stricter division of functions. Just as, in the relations between men and gods, Mitra takes "that which is well sacrificed" (that which, therefore, poses no question, since the ordinary mechanism of sacrifice suffices to guarantee its fruit), and Varuṇa "that which is badly sacrificed" (so as to punish the clumsy or ill-intentioned sacrificer), so, in the relations between men, Varuṇa the binder and Jupiter the avenger might have been involved at first with the oath as "avengers," whereas Mitra and Dius Fidius were "recorders" of the oath, or seen as the "drafters" of its terms. This, indeed, is what seems to emerge from the climactic formula of the *fetialis*, when the pact is concluded, in Livy, I, 24: Jupiter is invited to strike down the Romans if they are the first to break the conditions agreed to by both sides (*tu, illo die, populum Romanum sic ferito, et ego hunc porcum hic hodie feriam; tantoque magis ferito, quanto magis potes pollesque*: "on that day do thou, O Jupiter, so strike the Roman people as I shall here, this day, strike this swine; and do thou strike them so much the more, as thou art more able and more powerful").

Whatever the exact truth, however, these balances are unstable, and here again I raise the question of how the perspective can change according to whether one regards the divine couple from an internal viewpoint – each component then seen as defined by its opposition to the other – or from an external one, in which case the attributes specific to each component form a sum total, are combined in opposition to the rest of the universe and, if needs be, even concentrated entirely onto one of the two components, so as to form the complete figure of sovereignty.

Mitra, Numa and Blood Sacrifices

Numa is the "correct" sacrificer par excellence, the man of *fides*. Yet he meets his obligations with the least possible cost. Not only does he use cunning to substitute onions, hair and little fish for the human victim demanded by the terrible aspect of Jupiter, he also, Plutarch says, avoids making sacrifices that involve blood, limiting himself to offerings of flour, libations and "the least costly gifts" (*Numa*, 8). In particular, when he institutes the worship of Terminus, he refrains from sacrificing living beings because "enlightened by reason, he understood that the god of boundaries was a guardian of the peace and witness of just dealing, and should therefore be clear from slaughter" (*ibid.*, 16). This is one of the "scruples" that link the Numa of Roman legend with the Pythagorean sect. But we must be wary of supposing that it was artificially transferred from Pythagoras to Numa by moralistic historians, since it is a perfectly fitting characteristic for a typical king-priest hostile to all violence. By abstaining from the shedding of blood, Numa is simply embodying the extreme of his type.[8]

In India, on the divine level, a repugnance of the same kind is attributed to Mitra himself (*Śatapatha Brāhmaṇa*, IV, 1, 4, 8). The text in question is concerned with explaining a detail of the double offering termed *Maitrāvaruṇagraha*, in which milk (for Mitra) is mingled with soma (for Varuṇa): "Soma was Vṛtra; when the gods killed him they said to Mitra: 'Kill him, you also!' He would not, and said: 'I am the friend (*mitra*) of all things. . . .' 'We will exclude you from the sacrifice, then!' Then he said: 'I, too, kill him!' The animals drew away from Mitra, saying: 'He who was a friend, he has become an enemy (*amitra*). . . .' " So Mitra is opposed, by his nature at least, to blood sacrifice. He is hostile to all violence, even when it is sacred, because he is "friend" – and we need only restore the word's broad meaning in Indo-Iranian prehistory – that is, he is on the side of order, of agreement, of the peaceful settling of difficulties. But Vedic India could not condemn a form of sacrifice that its rituals demanded and that its brahmans, as much as the Roman flamines, practiced constantly. Consequently, Mitra "yielded," rather as the Romans, "after Numa," offering animal victims to the god of boundaries (Plutarch, *Numa*, 16). How could men, how could the gods, live without compromise, without concessions to the conventions?

On the human level, however, the Indian Manu, whose similarity to Numa we began to sketch earlier, and who is the hero of punctiliousness and good faith, of *satyam* and *śraddhā*, does not, to my knowledge, manifest any such repugnance to the shedding of blood. As we have seen, he was prepared to sacrifice his own wife. And yet we must remember that it was on the occasion of this cruel sacrifice, albeit certainly not by Manu's wish, that Indra lastingly, definitively, replaced the efficacy of the human victim with "the merit of intention." We should also bear in mind that extremely anodine oblation which plays an all-important role, sometimes in its own form and sometimes personified as a goddess, in both Manu's sacrificial and legislative activities. I refer, of course, to the *iḍā*, the offering he makes for the first time when the great flood, by "carrying away all creatures," has deprived him of the material for any other form of sacrifice. The *iḍā* consisted solely of water, clarified butter, whey, cream and curds; yet it was by the exclusive and repeated use of this powerful but bloodless offering that he repopulated an entire universe utterly laid waste.

Thus, it is not impossible that, from the very earliest times, one of the two magico-religious "systems" that served to explain and also to govern the universe (Mitra, Manu; Fides-Terminus, Numa) had oriented men's minds toward nonbloody forms of worship, while the other "system" (Varuṇa, Jupiter) had required the sacrifice of living beings, of animals or, occasionally, men. (It would not be too difficult, it seems to me, to reconcile these reflections with those of Jean Przyluski, *Revue de l'Histoire des Religions*, XCVI, 1927, p. 347ff.).

CHAPTER V

Ahura and Mithra

Iḍā and Egeria

For Manu, however, *Iḍā* (or *Iḷā*) is something far more than just an idyllic and powerful offering.

In the first place, it is the equivalent of *śraddhā*, as Sylvain Lévi has rightly stressed (*Doctrine du Sacrifice*..., p. 115): "The ideal type of the *śraddhādeva* in the *Brāhmaṇa* is precisely the ancestor of the human race, the model sacrificer, Manu. The bond that links Manu to *śraddhā* is so close and so strong that the memory of it has been perpetuated throughout the literature: the *Bhāgavata Purāṇa* refers to *śraddhā* as Manu's wife. The *Brāhmaṇa* translate this same idea into a different form: the feminine personage they associate with the Manu legend is *Iḍā*. *Iḍā*, in the language of the ritual, is a solemn offering that consists of four milk byproducts...; but the offering is so simple, and its effect so miraculous, that it deserves to be regarded as the perfect symbol of trust. The *iḍā* is *śraddhā*" (*Śatapatha Brāhmaṇa*, XI, 2, 7, 20: *śraddheḍā*; the text adds that he who "knows well that *iḍā* is *śraddhā* [*sa yo ha vai śraddheḍeti veda*] is assured of every success").

This trait is important. It establishes a link between bloodless offering and Manu's *śraddhā* as close as that which we found, in

Rome, between Numa's devotion and the innocence of his offerings: confirmation of what was stated at the end of the previous chapter. But there is more.

Iḍā is transmuted into a sort of demigoddess, and this supernatural being appears to Manu in the desolation that follows the deluge. "Through her" (by which we should understand, in this context, "by following her advice in the matter of sacrifice") he procreated that posterity which is "the posterity of Manu" (*Śatapatha Brāhmaṇa*, I, 8, 1, 10: *tayemāṃ prajātiṃ prajajñe yeyam Manoḥ prajātiḥ* – a unique piece of evidence, since we know that the flood story is not found elsewhere in the *Brāhmaṇa*). The text then adds: "Every blessing he called down through her was realized fully and entirely" (*ibid.*, *yām v enayā kāṃcāśisham āśāsta sāsmai sarvā samārdhyata*). In another story, which has several variations, *Iḍā* spies on the Asura (regarded as demonic) to see how they prepare their ritual fire, then on the technique used by the gods, and notes the failure of the first and the success of the second. Then "she said to Manu: I shall set up the fire for you in such a way that you will have abundance in your posterity and in your cattle, both male and female, and you will be made strong in this world, and you will conquer the world of heaven" (*Taittirīya Brāhmaṇa*, I, 1, 4, 7), and she then gives him detailed instructions as to the rites to be performed.

Iḍā is, in short, Manu's inspiration, his teacher, his Egeria. And that last word, used here in its everyday meaning, nevertheless points us toward the analogy between the tradition surrounding *Iḍā*, the demigoddess whose advice made the greatness of Manu, and the well-known tradition of Egeria, the demigoddess to whose counsels Numa owed the largest part of his wisdom, his knowledge, and his successes: a new and important point of contact between the two legislators. After he had lost his wife, Tatia, Numa preferred to live alone in the countryside, walking in the groves and meadows sacred to the gods. "It was said that if he thus fled from men, it was neither from melancholy nor grief. He had tasted the joy of a more august companionship and had been honored with a celestial marriage. The goddess (*δαίμονι*) Egeria loved him; and it was communion with her that gave him a life of blessedness and a wisdom more than human" (*εὐδαίμων ἀνὴρ χαὶ τὰ ϑεῖα πεπνυμένος γέγονεν*: Plutarch, *Numa*, 4).

Manu, Numa and Manius

And now we are touching on a divinity and a type of legend that must have been common among the Latins, since they are met with not only in Rome but also in Aricia. In fact, there is a nymph called Egeria who resides, as a secondary divinity, in the famous wood of Diana, where the *rex nemorensis* succumbed so frequently to his fate before encountering Frazer and immortality. And this Arician Egeria seems to be inseparable from a legendary personage who bears the same name and who is, in fact, the actual founder of the cult of Diana, the "dictator of the Latin league," Manius Egerius. This Manius was above all, famous for his descendants: there sprang so many Manii from him that this became the basis of a proverb which, to tell the truth, even the Romans were no longer certain they fully understood. In the *De significatione verborum* of Festus-Paulus, under *Manius*, we find: *Manius Egeri(us?)...nemorensem Dianae consecravit, a quo multi et clari viri orti sunt et per multos annos fuerunt* ("he consecrated the grove of Diana; from him many famous men sprang and lived many years"), and under *proverbium: multi Manii Ariciae* ("the many Manii of Aricia") (cf. Otto, *Sprichwörter der Römer*, p. 208ff.). One more certain element in this lacunary dossier is that pregnant women offered a sacrifice to "the nymph Egeria" in order to secure an easy delivery (Festus-Paulus, p. 67); so Egeria was as much a midwife as Manius Egerius was a procreator.

We do not know from what source Roman legend derived the name "Numa." Unexplained though its origin is, however, we should not be too hasty to say that it was Etruscan. Typologically, Numa is a Roman counterpart of the Indian Manu, the first man and the first king, who peopled the world with "the posterity of Manu" (*Manoḥ prajātiḥ*), which is to say, with men. Numa, like Manu, is the sacrificer and legislator par excellence, the hero of "trust," the founder of cults; and he is "inspired" by Egeria just as Manu is by *Iḍā*. Given all that, one is tempted to pay particular attention to Manius Egerius of Aricia, a political organizer, the founder of a cult, and, moreover, the ancestor of the proverbial multitude of the Manii. Might we not have here, in the pseudo-historical guise favored by Roman legend, not only the typological equivalent of Manu but even his phonetic near-equivalent? In fact, there is no reason to dissociate this Manius and these Manii from the *manes*, meaning "souls of the dead," or consequently from *Mania*, "mother or grandmother of dead souls" (Festus-Paulus, p. 115); from the *Maniae*, plural of *Mania*, denoting the *manes*, in the language of nurses, as larvae used to frighten the children in their care and, by extension, people of an unprepossessing appearance; or, lastly, from the *maniae* or *maniolae*, which are cakes in the shape of men (Festus, *ibid.*). Now, this entire series is evidence that the Latins were familiar with the stem *Mani-*, denoting, either on its own or through its derivatives, "dead men." And it so happens that Manius, the simple masculine form of the *Mania*, who is described as "*manium* (or *maniarum*) *avia materve*," is in fact the father and ancestor of innumerable Manii. More fortunate than the *manes* or *Maniae* of Rome, were these Manii of Aricia literally "men" in general, living men not yet passed into the state of *manes*? It is possible; and the difference would be slight. We know – from the Indo-Iranian Yama, if not from Manu himself – how closely contiguous or, more precisely, how continuous the notions of "first man" (first king, father of the human race) and "first dead man" (and thus king of the dead) were in practice.

The question remains open whether one can phonetically link this Latin **mani-* "(dead) man" and the **manu-* which, apart from the Sanskrit *Manu* (both the name and the common noun for "man"), has given, in particular, the Germanic *Mannus* (*-nn-* from **-nw-* regularly), mythical ancestor of the Germans (Tacitus), the Gothic *manna* "man" (genitive *mans*; stem **manw-*), and the Slavonic *mo*^{n}*žĭ* "man" (from **mangi-*, from accusative **manwi(n)*: A. Vaillant, *Revue des Etudes Slaves,* 1939, pp. 75-77), and of which we also have representatives in Phrygia (*Mávnσ*) and possibly in Armenia. (I am thinking of that legendary Saint *Mané* grotto into which Gregory the Illuminator withdraws and vanishes. Perhaps, in pagan times, it was a pathway to the other world, inhabited by a spirit of that other world?) It is only the differing quantities of the *-a-* in Latin **māni-* and Indo-European **mănu-* that present a difficulty, since the ending can be taken as just one more example of the well-known hesitations between stems in *-i-* and stems in *-u-* (cf. Cuny, *Revue de Philologie,* 1927, pp. 1-24). This link has already been proposed (see the state of the question in F. Muller Jzn, *Altitalisches Wörterbuch,* 1926, p. 254); but I do not propose to attach any more importance to it than it warrants, so that critics kind enough to take an interest in my work will not, I hope, regard this as a major structural element in my thesis.

Solar Dynasty and Lunar Dynasty: Ilā

If the two heavenly sovereigns, Mitra and Varuṇa, stand opposed not only as law and violence, not just as "brahman" par excellence and "leader of the Gandharva," but also as day and night, then it can come as no surprise to find on earth, in Indian epic "history," two dynasties of which one traces its ancestry back to the king-legislator Manu, and the other to the king-Gandharva Purūravas; one of which is called the "sun dynasty" (Manu being regarded as a descendant of the sun) and the other the "moon dynasty" (Purūravas being the grandson of the moon). These are the *sūryavaṃśaḥ* on the one hand, and the *candravaṃśaḥ* or *somavaṃśaḥ* on the other.

I recounted earlier the circumstances in which Purūravas was "initiated" into the world of the Gandharva, or "became one of the Gandharva." Thereafter, his life remained consonant with that beginning, and although it formed the basis for a variety of narratives, all of them have the same general sense (cf. Muir, *Original Sanskrit Texts*, I, 1868, p. 306ff.): supernatural powers, familiarity with animals and monsters, violent acts against the brahmans. In the first book of the *Mahābhārata* (75, 19ff.), for example, we find Purūravas reigning over thirteen ocean islands, surrounded by nonhuman beings, whereas he himself was a man of great fame (*amānushair vrtaḥ sarvair mānuṣaḥ san mahāyaśaḥ*). Then, intoxicated by his strength (*vīryonmattaḥ*), Purūravas entered into conflict with the brahmans and carried off their jewels despite their cries. Sanatkumāra came down from the world of Brahmā and addressed a warning to him, which he did not heed. Then, cursed by the angered *ṛṣi*, this greedy king, who had become drunk with his own strength and thus lost all sense (*balamadād naṣtasaṃjno narādhipaḥ*), perished. This tradition and others like it are interesting because they clarify the "morality of the Gandharva" in those times and social environments within which the terrestrial Gandharva operated. It is very similar to that of the first Luperci, Romulus and his uncouth companions, brigands, men of violence, reckless of rules and remonstrances alike, leading in this world the life of a feral world elsewhere. And Purūravas eventually perished as a result of his own excesses, cursed by the *ṛṣi*, by the Wise Men, as Roman Romulus was by the *senatores* he had not been afraid to defy. Nevertheless, Purūravas was far from being a "bad" or "wicked" king. Although the epics depict his behavior as excessive, and naturally take the side of the brahmans against him, he is no more condemned totally and outright than was Romulus, who had murdered his own brother and set himself against the Elders. Purūravas is in fact admired. One text even calls him *nṛdevaḥ* "the man-god" (*Harivaṃśa*, 8811).

The lunar dynasty, descended from Purūravas, proved worthy of its ancestor. Although Purūravas's own son, Ayus, is not remarkable except for his name ("vitality"), Ayus's son and successor Nahuṣa (whose name conceals a Semitic name for the snake: Sylvain Lévi, *Mémorial*..., pp. 316-318), is also destroyed by hubris, albeit only after a brilliant and just reign. So great was his prestige, in fact, that the gods at first summoned him to replace the vanished Indra at their head, and granted him the terrible gift of the "evil eye." Drunk with these unheard-of honors, however, the king harnessed the most venerable of his wise men to an aerial chariot and went riding through the sky, until, cursed by one of the wise men whom he had kicked, he fell to earth, struck by lightning, and was changed into a snake.

The solar dynasty is descended from Manu through his son Ikṣvāku. Although none of the princes who compose it reproduces the exceptionally priestly and exemplarily wise character of Manu, none, on the other hand, presents any "gandharvic" symptom. For our present purpose, in other words, Manu remains the only characterized element of the family.

The two dynasties are not entirely distinct. To be precise, it is the king-priest Manu's own daughter Ilā, who, having gone to reside with the moon god and having known the son of that god (the warlike Budha), gives birth to the first Gandharva-king, Purūravas, "Aila" Purūravas. This daughter, Ilā, is a figure with whom we are already acquainted. In the early ritualistic literature, in the archaic form of Iḍā or Iḷā, she is in fact Manu's "daughter" and Egeria, as well as the personification of his oblation. In the epic literature – doubtless inheriting features from extra-priestly traditions (although Purūravas is already qualified as Aila in *Ṛg Veda*, X, 95, 18) – she has a different character and cuts a rather different figure (cf. Johannes Hertel, *Die Geburt des Purūravas, Wiener Zeitschrift für die Kunde des Morgenlandes*, XXV, 1911, pp. 153-186). One constant tradition has it that after journeying to visit the moon god, she was obliged to change sex several times; some texts assert that she thereafter continued to change sex every month. According to the *Liṅga Purāṇa* (I, 65, 19), she was even transformed into a *Kimpuruṣa*, which is to say into a monster, half-horse and half-man, a variety, already, of Gandharva. Thus, through Ilā, Manu's daughter, a direct line of communication is established between the sun dynasty and the moon dynasty, between the "wise" and the "tumultuous," between the king-priest and the race of Gandharva-kings.

Roman Kings: The Pious Line and the Warlike Line: Ilia

We have no means of interpreting this curious tradition, but it is interesting to rediscover it in Rome. The analogy is very striking, even down to its details, if we follow a number of exegists in their opinion that Numitor, the "good" king of Alba and grandfather of Romulus, is a doublet of Numa.

The list of Rome's first kings contrasts and alternates war-loving, terrible kings with pious, peace-loving kings:[1] the former are Romulus and Tullus Hostilius, who was a descendant of one of Romulus's principal lieutenants; the latter are Numa and his grandson, Ancus Marcius. Tullus Hostilius, Numa's successor, met a fate even more tragic than that of Romulus, and quite as tragic as that of Nahuṣa, even though his reign had earned the qualification *egregium*. He mocked his predecessor's finest institutions, above all his piety to the gods, which he (Tullus) presumptuously (*καθυβρίσας*) accused of making men cowardly and effeminate. In this way he directed the minds of the Romans toward war. "But this imprudent temerity did not last long: seized by a grave and mysterious illness, which troubled his reason, he fell into a superstition that was far removed from the piety of Numa... and he died by a stroke of lightning" (Plutarch, *Numa*, 22).[2] On the other hand, Ancus Marcius, the son of Numa's daughter and *gloriae avitae memor*, was primarily concerned to restore, in all their rigor and purity, the religious customs that Tullus had flouted (Livy, I, 32). Thus the Romulus-Numa opposition continued after them. In Ancus's case we can speak quite literally of "dynasty," and in that of Tullus there is at least moral "filiation," since he is descended from one of Romulus's most typical henchmen. Moreover, these two lines stand in the same typological relationship to one another as the first representatives of the moon dynasty and the ancestor of the sun dynasty in India.

Now, we know how Romulus came to be born: the true daughter of the wise Numitor, a Vestal, had been impregnated by a god, by Mars, and the blood of that warlike god, mingled with the human blood of Numitor, produced the future king-Lupercus, the child who was to be suckled by the she-wolf and formed by a childhood in the wilderness. And that daughter of Numitor, "functionally" symmetrical to the Indian Ilā, daughter of Manu, is called Ilia.

Mithra and Ahura-Mazdāh, Mihrjān and Naurōz

In Iran, where the facts are more confused, and where one senses the purposeful hand of the reformers even in the earliest texts, I shall leave it to the specialists to prospect in their own territory. The Uppsala school, inspired by Mr. Nyberg, is already addressing itself, with happy results, to this question of the sovereign god (G. Widengren, *Hochgottglaube im alten Iran, Uppsala Univ. Aarsskrift*, 1938, VI). I shall therefore limit myself to a few observations made in the light of the Indian and Roman material we have been examining.[3]

It is certainly important, from a historical point of view, to record the ups and downs of Mithra's career; to note, for example, that he is absent from the *Gāthās* and to determine how he found his way back into the other parts of the Avesta. But the details of such misfortunes tell the comparatist very little, since his task is to search through the documents, of whatever kind, from any era and any source, for vestiges of the early state of the Indo-Iranian couple

*Mitra-*Varuṇa, already present in the Mitani list of gods and so well preserved in India.[4] I have already referred, in this context, to the customary Avestic formula *Mithra-Ahura*, which, associating Mithra as it does with a "supreme Ahura" on an equal footing, is certainly anterior to Mazdaism proper. Is Ahura-Mazdāh the heir of this "preeminent Ahura" and, consequently, homologous with Varuṇa, the great Vedic Asura? This hypothesis, long accepted without argument, has subsequently been hotly disputed – wrongly, in my belief. On this point I regret being in disagreement with a mythologist of such standing as H. Lommel, but, since all my research has fully confirmed the validity of the description "sovereign" as applied to the Asura Varuṇa by Bergaigne, it seems to me more than probable that the rise of Ahura-Mazdāh derives precisely from the fact that he was an extension of the sovereign god of the premazdeans. The work of the Iranian reformers would then have consisted in a successful attempt to improve the morals of this ancient sorcerer, on the one hand, and, on the other, to isolate him in a position far above all other divine entities (cf. my *Ouranos-Varuṇa*, pp. 101-102).[5]

One consideration concerning Mithra strengthens this opinion still further. It is a fact that a religion's great annual festivals are less easily reformed than its dogmas. It is therefore probable that, like Christianity in other times and other places, Mazdaism was simply "sanctifying" the previous state of affairs when it balanced its year on two great festivals separated by the maximum interval (spring equinox to autumn equinox) and clearly antithetical in their meaning and their myths. And those festivals are placed under two invocations, one of Ahura-Mazdāh, the other of Mithra.

On the cosmic level, Naurōz, the Persian New Year and feast of Ahura-Mazdāh, celebrated "on the day Ohrmazd" of the first month, commemorates creation. The feast of Mithra (*Mithrakāna, Mihragān, Mihrjān*...), celebrated on "the day Mihr" in "the month Mihr," prefigures the end of the world. Why is this? Albiruni replies (*The Chro-*

nology of Ancient Nations, 1879, p. 208): "Because, at Mihrjān, that which believes attains its perfection and has no more matter left to believe more, and because the animals cease to couple; at Naurōz it is the exact opposite." In this opposition between immobilized perfection and creative force, there is no difficulty in recognizing the theological adaptation of an old law-magic, conservation-fecundity opposition that we have seen expressed in India by the couple Mitra-Varuṇa and in Rome – even apart from the opposite and complementary activities of flamines and Luperci – by Numa "perfecting" the "creation" of Romulus. There is an even more precise correspondence, however: this division of seasonal roles (the beginning of winter, the beginning of summer) between Ahura-Mazdāh and Mithra, in accordance with the "faculty of growth" and the "arrest of growth" that they express, clearly rests on the same symbolism as the assimilation of Mitra to the waning moon and Varuṇa to the waxing moon, which has sometimes been rather overhastily attributed to the "fancy" of brahman authors.

In epic terms, Naurōz was instituted by Yim (Yama), a king whose carnivalesque features leap to the eye, and who is specifically thought of as the father of the monster Gandarep (Gandarəva), just as the Vedic Yama is said to be the son of the Gandharva. Mihrjān, on the contrary, was instituted by Faridūn (Thraetaonoa), a law-abiding hero, who reestablished justice and morality after the tyrannical masquerade of the monster Aždahāk (Azhi-Dahāka), for whom Kndrv (again Gandarəva) acted as steward of royal entertainment. Here, once again, we find the distinction so clearly made in India between a "moon dynasty" and a "sun dynasty," between Gandharva kings (Purūravas, Nahuṣa) and the legislator king (Manu).

This comparison is reinforced even further by the fact that Yim's acting out of his triumph, commemorated annually during Naurōz, coincides exactly with that of Nahuṣa: he harnesses *devs* to an aerial chariot and has himself carried at tremendous speed through the sky;

and men, "praising God for having raised their king to such a degree of greatness and power," institute this annual feast (Al Tha'ālibī, *Histoire des Rois de Perse*, trans. Zotenberg, p. 13). The scene commemorated by Mihrjān, on the contrary, is one of calm and serenity: Faridūn, having driven out Aždahāk, seats himself upon the throne, surrounded "near and far" by his vassals, and gives an audience to his people. "His physiognomy was illumined, from his mouth fell gracious words, the reflection of his divine majesty shone within him," and his subjects founded the feast of Mihrjān "to express that they had recovered through his justice the life that they had lost...." Here we recognize a set of oppositions only too familiar by now: *celeritas* and *gravitas*, violent triumph and ordered organization, powerful king and just king.

These systems of antithetical representations, linked by a deeply rooted tradition to the two complementary feasts of Ahura-Mazdāh and Mithra – at the two equinoxes – seem to me to confirm that, before reform, the couple Mithra-Ahura had the same meaning, the same double orientation, the same balance, as the Vedic couple Mitra-Varuṇa, and that, consequently, the Ahurah Mazdāh of the Avesta is to be linked, typologically and genetically, with the Vedic Varuṇa.

Chapter VI

Nexum and Mutuum

Romulus as Binder

Varuṇa is the "binder." Whoever respects *satyam* and *śraddhā* (in other words, the various forms of correct behavior) is protected by Mitra, but whoever sins against them is immediately bound, in the most literal sense of the word, by Varuṇa. I have pointed out elsewhere that the Greek Uranos is also a "binder," even though his "binding" lacks any moral value.[1] Uranos does not enter into combat any more than Varuṇa does. Like Varuṇa, he seizes whomsoever he wishes, and he "binds" him. Once in his grasp, there is no possibility of resistance. The rituals and the fabulous "history" of the Romans retain, in the expected places, vestiges of these same representations.

The flamen dialis is an "unbinder": any man in chains who takes refuge with him is immediately set free, and his chains thrown from the house, not through the window but from the roof (Aulus Gellius, X, 15 : *vinclum, si aedes eius introierit, solui necessum est et vincula par impluvium in tegulas subduci atque inde foras in viam demitti*; cf. Plutarch, *Roman Questions*, 111). Moreover, if a man condemned to be beaten with rods falls in supplication at his feet, then it is forbidden to beat him that day (*ibid., si quis ad verberandum ducatur,* *si ad pedes eius supplex procubuerit, eo die verberari piaculum est*). These two interdependent privileges make the flamen dialis the exact opposite of a cog in the machinery of "terrible kingship," and of Romulus (or other kings of his type, such as Tullus Hostilius or Tarquin, to whom the institution of the *lictores* is sometimes attributed). Always accompanying Romulus, according to Plutarch (*Romulus*, 26), were "men with staves, keeping off the populace, and they were girt with thongs with which to bind at once those he ordered to be bound" (*ἐβάδιζον δὲ πρόσθεν ἕτεροι Βακτηρίαις ἀνείργοντες τὒν ὄχλον, ὑπεζωσμένοι δ' ἱμάντας ὥστε συνδεῖν εὐθὺς οὕς προστάξειε*). This, Plutarch says, is the origin of the *lictores*, whose name derives from *ligare* (cf. *Roman Questions*, 67). And there is no reason to reject this link sensed by the ancients between *lictor* and *ligare*: *lictor* could well be formed on a radical verb **ligere*, for which no evidence has survived, which would stand in the same relation to *ligare* as *dicere* to *dicare* (cf. Ernout-Meillet, *Dictionary of Latin Etymology*). Romulus, then, in direct contrast to the flamen dialis, was a binder and also a flogger, since his escort carries both kinds of weapon and since the lictors of the historical era carried the *virga* in addition to their *fasces*. This group of representations would seem to merit closer scrutiny: indeed, it does seem, both in the Romulus legend and in the rituals derived from it, that *lictores*, Celeres and Luperci are all closely related notions. In particular, the equipment of the first lictors is also that of the historical Luperci, who were belted with leather straps and used them as whips.

Since the essential nature of the flamen dialis is, in the highest degree, anti-binding, it becomes easy to understand why the flamen dialis should be a very heavily clothed man who must never wear any kind of knot, either in his hair, his belt or anywhere about him (*nodum in apice neque in cinctu neque in alia parte ullum habet*, Aulus Gellius, X, 15), whereas the Luperci are naked men "girt" with straps; and why the Luperces, as *equites*, necessarily wear a ring, whereas the flamen dialis only has the right to "mock rings," that are broken and hollow (*annulo uti, nisi pervio cassoque, fas non est*; Aulus Gellius, X, 15).

An analogous interplay of representations occurs, put to rather more subtle use, in India. In the *Śatapatha Brāhmaṇa* (III, 2, 4, 18) we read, for example, that if one speaks the formula "May Mitra fasten you by the foot" at the moment a sacrificial cow is fastened, it is for the following reason: "The rope assuredly belongs to Varuṇa. If the cow were bound (without any special formula) with a rope, then she would become the thing of Varuṇa. If she were not fastened at all, on the other hand, she would not be controllable. But that which is Mitra's is not Varuṇa's...." The trick is clear enough: as long as the necessary bond is put on the cow by a god other than the special divinity of binding, the risk of automatic confiscation is avoided. And if that office is entrusted to Mitra, Varuṇa's complement in the order of things, that is enough to avoid the danger of any counter-offensive, any attempt on Varuṇa's part to claim a share of the sacrifice. Such ruses are customary in India (cf. in my *Flāmen-brahman*, pp. 62-63, the "brahmanic" ruse adopted with regard to the Roman rule that requires the flaminica to be a woman, *univira*, one who has had no other husband before the flamen).

Mitra, Varuna and Debts

It is natural that the punctiliousness over which the Mitra-Varuṇa couple presides should be religious in nature. But the very name "Mitra," as well as the value of personified "contract" that the Avestic Mithra clearly possesses, attests that even in prehistory this god's activity extended beyond the realm of ritual and sacrifice. In addition, the *Ṛg Veda* hymns, as Meillet points out, contain more than vestiges of the specifically juridical values attributed to Mitra and also, interdependently with him, to Varuṇa. In particular, these two gods have a link with debts. They are termed – along with the Āditya as a whole – *cayamānā ṛṇāni* (*Ṛg Veda*, II, 27, 4), "those who collect, gather in, exact repayment of, debts." And it has been observed that the activity proper to Mitra is expressed by an obscure verb that lawyers have finally managed to elucidate: the causative of the root *yat-*. With reference to a textual variant in Manu (VIII, 158) and to the word *vairayātana* (cf. later *vairaniryātana* with the meaning "revenge, vengeance"), which originally meant "settlement, payment (*yātana*) for hostility or, rather, of a man's price (*vaira-*)," J. Jolly (*Beiträge zur indischen Rechtsgeschichte, Zeitsch. d. deutsch. morgenl. Gesellschaft*, XLIV, 1890, pp. 339-340) has suggested that this causative *yātay-* should be translated as "to see that something is paid back" (in accordance with a custom or a contract; cf. Old Scand. *gjalda*, etc.), which is more or less what Meillet has done in his article in the 1907 *Journal Asiatique*. There, Mitra is qualified (*Ṛg Veda*, III, 59, 5; VIII, 102, 12) as *yātayaj-janaḥ*, "who sees that men are paid back." This epithet also appears (*ibid.*, V, 72, 2) applied to Mitra and to Varuṇa in a context dominated by the words *vrata* ("law") and *dharman* ("rule") (*vratena stho dhruvakṣemā dharmaṇā yātayaj- janā*: "with the law you are firmly established, with the rule you are those who make men fulfill their commitments," Meillet translates). I am not sufficiently informed about the regulations governing debts at the time of the Vedic hymns to comment on these terms. However, we are assured (Pischel and Geldner, *Vedische Studien*, I, p. 288) that insolvent debtors were "bound" by the same token as those lax in sacrifice, and doubtless in a more material sense. As the ritualistic literature repeats to satiety, bonds belong to Varuṇa. Once more, then, we glimpse a collaboration between Mitra and Varuṇa, the former presiding benevolently over correctly executed exchanges, the latter "binding" any defaulters. And various texts do suggest, with differing nuances, a functional division of this kind: M. Filliozat has brought to my attention, for example, *Kathaka*, XXVII, 4 (ed. L. v. Schroeder, 1909, p. 142, 1, 9-13): *imāḥ prajā mitreṇa śāntā varuṇena vidhṛtāḥ* "the creatures were *calmed* by Mitra, *held in check* by Varuṇa."[2]

The Nexum and the Mutuum[3]

It is impossible not to be reminded here of one of the earliest fragments of Roman law, one that has come down to us as scarcely more than a memory and moreover stripped of any religious element. Although Jupiter and Fides were probably involved in these transactions at one time, this had been forgotten before the earliest documents; nor is it surprising that the material takes the form it does in a land that had successfully separated its law from its religion as early as prehistoric times.

I am referring to the very earliest system of debt, dominated by two words *nexum* and *mutuum*. The first is derived from the conjugation of the verb *necto-nexus*, "I bind-bound" (remodeled on *plecto-plexus*, from the root **nedh-*, "to bind," which is also that of *nodus*, "knot," Sanskrit *naddha-*, "fastened," Irish *naidim*, "I bind": Meillet-Ernout, *Dictionnaire étymologique latin*). The second is formed on the very same root, **mei-*, "make exchanges (of the potlatch type)" that also gave us *Mitra*; and the form *mutuus* must be early, since Indo-Iranian (Sanskrit *mithuna*, Avestic *mithvara*, *mithvana* "pair"; Sanskrit *maithuna*, "union, coitus, marriage") and Balto-Slavonic (Old Slavonic *mitusĭ*, "alternatively," Lettish *miêtus*, "exchange") also have derivatives in *-t-u-* from this root. *Mutuum* is, literally, (*aes*) *mutuum*, "the money borrowed," and also "borrowing." *Nexum* is the state of the *nexus*, of the insolvent debtor who was, very literally, bound and subjugated by the creditor. Latin is the only Indo-European language in which the vocabulary of debt is constituted by such clear-cut terms. And it is doubtless no mere chance that we are able to recognize here, in two coupled, abstract words, a strict equivalent of the exchange-god Mitra (with the same root) and the binder-god Varuṇa (with the same image).

It has often been pointed out, with regard to the *nexum*, that it is the most ancient form of relation between the man who gives (or lends?) and the man who receives; and stress has often been laid on its mechanical, inhuman character, which contrasts so strongly with the casuistic direction taken by later law, and reminds us rather of the rigor and the automatic nature of magic transactions. Perhaps we are not quite so far from the sacred as I assumed a moment ago; and when Livy terms this system *ingens vinculum fidei* – using two words that are semantic neighbors of *nexum* and *mutuum* – perhaps he is conjuring up, behind the human legal procedure and as its foundation, the ancient Fides coupled with some divine and terrible "lictor."

Legal historians, however, do not agree on the relation between the two terms. For some, *nexum* and *mutuum* denote two successive phases in the development of a single mechanism. For others, they denote two distinct mechanisms contemporary with one another but opposed in their mode and point of application. I shall take care to offer no opinion either way. It will be sufficient if I observe that in both hypotheses, even in the first (and it is, naturally, on the first that I lay stress here, since it is the only one that could make for difficulties), we are dealing with two "coupled" notions that are interdependent in the second case and parallel in the first.

It is accepted in the first hypothesis that the *mutuum* is not a new mechanism that replaced an earlier one, called *nexum*. Rather, it is seen as a later name given to a system first called *nexum*; and it is generally accepted that *mutuum* was substituted for *nexum* simultaneously with the first attenuation of that cruel mechanism, and at a time – another progressive step – when the mechanism was extended from the *ius civile* to the *ius gentium*. All this is possible. But, even if this evolution is accepted, we may merely be dealing with one of those illusory factual details that abounds in the "early days" of all forms of Roman history, whether political, religious or legal.

It is undoubtedly the case that it is by extension alone that *mutuum* could have become the *nomen* of the legal act, of the contract, for which *nexum* already provided a perfectly adequate *nomen*. For, as we have seen, *mutuum* is the *res* borrowed; it is the material of the act and not the act itself. Thus I am quite disposed to accept, if the texts indicate such a conclusion, that *mutuum* replaced *nexum* at a time when the terrible aspects of the act had been eliminated or greatly softened (very early, it seems, since the process was in any case complete by the fourth century B.C.). But that would not entitle us to ignore the fact that there must always have been, even during those times when the *nexum* was at its strictest, a "material" involved in the contractual act, and that this material must in fact have been called *mutuum*, since the word is Indo-European, archaic in form, and denotes "the thing exchanged," not metaphorically but directly by its very root. Thus the coupled notions *nexum-mutuum*, whatever their subsequent history, originally will have denoted the two components of the mechanism – a mechanism that will then have been successively denoted by first one, and then the other of the two terms, according to whether it was the "violent" or, later on, the "juridical" element proper that was dominant. To this observation I shall add one more. Historians often argue as though the beginnings of Roman law were an absolute beginning. Yet before the *aes mutuum*, even before the *aes* itself, there surely must have been contracts (at least constraining gifts, exchanges, potlatches, all those things expressed by the root, **mei-*); likewise, those earlier juridico-religious acts must have involved some material element. It is not by chance that *pecunia* is derived from *pecus*. When the pastoral Indo-Europeans invaded Latium, the *mutuum*, "the thing given with – obligatory – duty to reciprocate" (later: "the thing lent"), normally must have been an animal or animals. At this point, I would like to draw attention to the epithet applied in the Avesta to *Mithra: vourugaoyaoitis* (cf. Vedic *gavyuti*, which seems to denote a certain acreage of pasture), and also to verse 86 of the *Yast* of *Mithra* in which, in a list of human beings likely to invoke that god and summon him to their aid (leaders of countries, provinces, etc.), there suddenly appears from among all the nonhuman creatures, a lone cow which is "imprisoned" and presumably stolen: "Who, she asks, will take us back to the byre?"[4] In other words, however archaic such procedures as that carried out *per aes et libram* might now seem in relation to later Roman civilization, it is likely that they originally appeared as innovations in relation to such early pastoral traditions.

The authors who accept the second hypothesis relating to *nexum* and *mutuum*, either sociologists or writers influenced by sociology, do not hesitate to restore a magical or quasi-magical value to the *nexum* (Popescu-Spineni, *Die Unzulässigkeit des Nexum als Kontrakt*, Iassi, 1931, cf. *Zeitsch. der Savigny-Stiftung*, 1933, p. 527ff.; H. Lévy-Bruhl, *Nexum et mancipatio*, in *Quelques problèmes...*, 1934, p. 139ff.; Pierre Noailles, *Nexum*, in *Rev. histor. du droit français et étranger*, 1940-1941, p. 205ff.; Raymond Monier, *Manuel élémentaire de droit romain*, II (3rd ed.), *les Obligations*, 1944, p. 13ff.; cf. Marcel Mauss, *The Gift*, p. 47ff., and the work of Huvelin mentioned on Mauss's p. 117, n. 3). They sometimes go so far as to dispute that the *nexum* is in fact a true contract, but in any case regard it as a radically different type of commitment from that of the *mutuum*; and different, as I indicated, not merely in its form but also in its area of application. According to this view, the operation of the *nexum* presupposes the coexistence of men both free and of very different levels (as regards both wealth and status), whereas the *mutuum* is seen as functioning between equals (between "friends," Monier says on p. 21). By means of the *nexum*, a *humilis* would bind himself to a *potens* and would accept bond-service of some kind, because no more-balanced form of exchange is conceivable between them. By means of the *mutuum*, one *aequalis* would render some service to another, either without payment or with the understanding of a –

theoretically free – return. If we accept this hypothesis, then we are led to conceive of two early types of contractual law – according to whether economic relations are being established between classes or within a single social class – both equally far removed, but in opposite directions, from traditional law, and defining it in advance by that very gap between them: a terrible law and a flexible law, a magic law and a trusting law. This would imply a particular Roman utilization, with the division occurring *between two possible types of social relation*, of the dualist system that occurs in Vedic India with no (apparent) distinction in its social application, but with a division *between the two possible attitudes of the debtor* (Mitra protecting the good debtor who repays, Varuṇa seizing the bad debtor). But perhaps this interpretation of the Roman facts is too simple, since it does in fact appear that it was the bad debtor only – himself, and doubtless also his wife and his children *in manu* – who was *nexus*. In other words, the *nexum*, the "binding," the subjugation, happened only after a default on repayment had occurred, and we remain uncertain about the state that followed the making of the commitment and preceded defalcation.

That, at least is what seems to emerge from the accounts of historians, for it is naturally to the historical or pseudo-historical traditions that we must turn in order to gain some idea of how this archaic mechanism functioned. For example, we need to re-read Livy's account of the abolition of the *nexum* (VIII, 28): in the last quarter of the fourth century B.C., a libidinous creditor wished to abuse a handsome youth who, as a result of debts contracted by the boy's father, was in his household as a *nexus*. The young man resisted, and the master, having run out of threats, had him stripped naked and whipped. The victim ran out of the house and aroused the people in his defense. The consuls convoked the senate, and a law was voted on the spot. "On that day," Livy tells us, "through the criminal act and abuse of a single man, the awesome bond of *fides* (*ingens vinculum fidei*) was vanquished. By order of the senate, the consuls announced to the people that no man, unless as the result of a merited sentence and while awaiting punishment, should thenceforward be held in shackles or bonds, and that in the future it should be the property and not the body of the debtor that should be answerable for money borrowed (*pecuniae creditae*). Thus it was that the 'bound' (*nexi*) were 'unbound' (*soluti*). And measures were taken to see that they should not be bound in future (*cautumque in posterum ne necterentur*)."

Indra Against the Bonds of Varuṇa

For our purposes, another passage from Livy (II, 23-24) is even more important. It belongs to that group of epic narratives describing the wars of the early Republic against its neighbors. In a different way, but for the same reason, these stories are as much charged with "mythology" as the traditional accounts of the city's kings, in the sense that they illustrate and justify, if not actual festivals and cults, at least those law-abiding forms of behavior and those moral constants of the historical era to which the Romans adhered at least as firmly as to their religion. But in order to evaluate this document correctly, we first need to return to the India of the brahmans.

There, with the exception of the allusions to debt mentioned a little earlier, the material we have to deal with is of a magico-religious nature, or what one might venture to term "ritual law," that is, the rules that regulate exchanges between sacrificers and gods. As we have seen, the guarantors of this law are Mitra and Varuṇa, and the clumsy or fraudulent sacrificer runs the risk of being "bound" promptly by Varuṇa, just as, in ancient Rome, the defaulting debtor automatically became *nexus* in the household of his creditor. But the *Brāhmaṇa* recount several stories in which a sacrificer escapes from this gloomy situation thanks to an unexpected intervention. These incidents merit investigation.

I have already cited the first: it is the story of Manu, slave to *śraddhā*, preparing to sacrifice his wife on the demand of two demonic priests. The fatal mechanism is set in motion, inevitable and blind: if Manu does not go through with it to the end, if he succumbs for an instant to his humanity, then he transgresses the law of sacrifice and falls prey to the bonds of Varuṇa. In fact, he doesn't waver: he is going to go through with it. And then another god steps in, one who is neither Mitra nor Varuṇa, a god who feels pity and who decides, having taken the initiative and the responsibility of slicing through this terrible dilemma, that the sacrifice shall not in fact take place and that Manu shall still secure the benefit of it. That god is Indra.

The second story to place on file is that of Śunaḥśepa, which is also important in other respects. A king has been "seized" by Varuṇa and stricken with dropsy because he did not keep his cruel promise to sacrifice his own son to the god. Varuṇa eventually consents to a substitution; but, whatever happens, he wants a human victim equal or superior to the prince. And that is how the young brahman Śunaḥśepa, duly bought and bound to the stake, comes to await his death in accordance with the ritual of rājasūya (royal consecration), especially revealed by Varuṇa on this occasion. In order to escape his death, Śunaḥśepa prays to various gods; first to Prajāpati, who passes him on to Agni, who passes him on to Savitṛ, who sends him back to Varuṇa: "It is by the king Varuṇa that you are bound," he tells the young man, "go to him!" Varuṇa listens to him, but, as is the way with great specialists imprisoned by their own technique, the god apparently can do nothing to help the person he has bound. The young man addresses himself once more to Agni, who sends him to the Viśve Devāḥ, who in their turn send him to Indra, who sends him to the Aśvin, who tell him to pray to Dawn. And the miracle occurs: stanza by stanza, as he prays, Varuṇa's "bonds" which hold the king fall away; his dropsy disappears; and there is no further need of a victim. In this story the "savior gods" are numerous, and Indra's role is not as clear-cut as in the previous one; though at least he is well placed beside those beneficient and noncombatant divinities the Aśvin. And doubtless his intervention was more decisive still in the less "priestly" forms of the story, since later writings were to contrast the ancient ritual of royal consecration instituted by Varuṇa (*rājasūya*), stained from the first by human blood (as the Śunaḥśepa story presupposes and several details confirm), with that which has no human victim, instituted by Indra (*aśvamedha*). I am thinking here, in particular, of Chapter 83 of Book VII of the *Rāmāyana*, in which Rāma, preparing to celebrate *rājasūya*, is dissuaded by his brother. "How could you carry out such a sacrifice, O Prince," the latter asks him, "one in which we see the extermination, here on earth, of the royal line? And those heroes, O King, who have achieved their heroism here on earth, it will be destruction for them, all of them, below, and a cause for universal anger (*sa tvam evaṃvidham yajnam arhitāsi kathaṃ nṛpa pṛthivyāṃ rājavaṃsānāṃ vināśo yatra dṛśyate? pṛthivyāṃ ye ca puruṣā rājan pauruṣam āgatāḥ sarveṣam bhāvita tatra samkṣayaḥ sarvakopajaḥ*, slokas 13-14). The implications here are clear: the classic ritual of *rājasūya* simulated – and thus once required in reality – the killing of the *rājanya*, nobles who are related to the king. Happily, however, Rāma yields to his brother's argument and unhesitatingly renounces "the greatest of all the sacrifices, the *rājasūya* (*rājasūyat krāttutamāt nivartayāmi*)," because "an act detrimental to the world ought not be performed by wise men (*lokapīḍākaraṃ karma na kartavyaṃ vicakṣaṇaiḥ*)." In its place he celebrates the no less efficacious, no less glorious *aśvamedha*, that very *aśvamedha*, respectful of human life, originally instituted by Indra.

The Morality of the Sovereign and the Morality of the Hero

An attempt to explore fully the import of these interventions by Indra would explode the entire framework of this present work. Indra, the warrior-god, first among his brothers the Marut, leader of a band of heroes, is set here in opposition to Varuṇa the magician, king of the Gandharva. We are no longer in the realm of mythology proper to the sovereign-priest, but rather at that point of high drama where it mingles violently with the mythology of the military leader. We are passing from one "social function" and – since this is India – from one "social class" to another, and consequently from one morality, one law, one *Weltanschauung* to another. Sociological research on the Marut, the Indo-Iranian "society of warriors," has been set in motion by Stig Wikander (*Der arische Männerbund*, Lund-Upsal, 1938) and is to be pursued. For the moment, however, the evidence is not clearest in the Indo-Iranian world, but in the Germanic world, and it is not by chance that Wikander's work is inspired by Otto Höfler's *Kultische Geheimbünde der Germanen* (Frankfurt-am-Main, 1934). I have also sketched in a number of links between the two domains in Chapters VI and VII of *Mythes et dieux des Germains* (Paris, Leroux, 1939. See, in particular, p. 93n., pp. 97, 102ff.; and Chapter X, "*Census iners*..."). What emerges from the evidence as a whole (even as early as Tacitus, *Germania*, 31) is that the economic morality of such warrior groupings, as well as their sexual morality and conduct in general, both in peace and in war, had nothing in common with principles regulating the rest of society. "None of them," Tacitus tells us (*loc. cit.*), describing the "military society" of the Chatti, "has house, or land, or any business; wherever they present themselves they are entertained, wasteful of the substance of others, indifferent to personal possessions..." (*nulli domus aut ager aut aliqua cura; prout ad quemque venere, aluntur, prodigi alieni, contemptores sui*...). It is not difficult to perceive from this how distant such societies were from Mitra and Varuṇa – from all "punctiliousness," from all mechanisms of the *nexum* and even the *mutuum* types, from any system of property, debts, loans. And it becomes easier to understand how one of the most forceful texts that Wikander has found in the Avesta – directed against the *mairya-*, in whom he rightly recognizes the members of an Iranian Männerbund and not mere "bandits" (as Darmesteter translates the term, *Zend-Avesta*, II, p. 445) – presents such groups as the archetypal *mithrō-drug-*, those, in other words, "who violate contracts" on the human level and those "who lie to Mithra" on the divine level. This text, which actually occurs at the beginning of the great *Yast* of *Mithra* (*Yast*, X, 2), is the fossilized evidence, as it were, of very early conflicts between the moralities and religions of society's first two "functions" and "classes."

It should come as no surprise that the god of these "societies of men," even though they are "terrible" in so many respects, figures in Indian fable – in opposition to the binder-magician – as a merciful god, as the god who unfetters Varuṇa's (legally) bound victims; for the warrior and the sorcerer alike or, on another level, the soldier and the policeman, make inroads when necessary on the life and liberty of their fellow man, but each operates in accordance with procedures that the other finds repugnant. And the warrior especially, because of his position either on the fringe of or even above the code, regards himself as having the right to clemency; the right to break, among other things, the mandates of "strict justice"; the right, in short, to introduce into the terrible determinism of human relations that miracle: humanity. To the old principle that can be formulated as *ius nullum nisi summum*, he at least dares to substitute something that already resembles the principle that we still revere while often ignoring it in practice: *summum ius summa iniuria*. Having studied the same phenomenon in the Chinese domain, Marcel Granet has accustomed us, in lectures and books alike, to watch for, to weigh the significance of what one might term the "advent of the warrior." Throughout the world this revolution signals one of the great moments, constitutes one of the great openings of societies to progress. The Indian traditions we have been dealing with here belong to this general category, as does, I believe, the inspiring legend recounted in Livy, II, 23-24, which does not, naturally enough, take place between men and gods (as in India), and in which it is no longer religious and liturgical debts that are at stake but legal and pecuniary debts. It is a story of creditors, debtors and soldiers.

Military Oath Versus Nexum

War against the Volscii is imminent, and Rome is torn apart by hatreds engendered by its laws governing debt. "We are fighting abroad for freedom and empire," the indignant *nexi* cry, "and in Rome itself we are seized and oppressed (*captos et oppressos esse*) by our fellow citizens!" The city rumbles with unrest, and then an incident occurs that precipitates the storm. An old man in rags, pale, exhausted, wild-eyed, hair and beard in disarray, hurls himself into the forum. He is recognized as a former centurion. He displays his chest, covered with wounds earned in many battles and he gives voice to his misfortunes. He has been forced into debt since the enemy laid waste his land. Swollen by the interest rates levied upon them, those debts have stripped him, successively, of the field handed down to him by his father and his grandfather, of all his goods and of his freedom itself (*velut tabem pervenisse ad corpus*). He has been removed from his home by his creditor, and placed not merely into bond-service but thrust into a veritable prison, into a place of execution (*non in servitium, sed in ergastulum et carnificinam*). Finally, he shows his back, bloody from recent blows. A riot breaks out. Those who are currently *nexi*, as well as those who have been in the past (*nexu vincti solutique*), rush from all sides to the scene, invoking the *fides Quiritium*. The senators are besieged and threatened; they would be massacred but for the consuls who intervene. The people refuse to be pacified until a consul, learning that a formidable Volscian army is on the march, imposes the following decision upon the senate: "No man must detain a Roman citizen, either in chains or in prison, so as to hinder him from enrolling his name before the consuls (*nominis edendi apud consules potestas*). And nobody may either seize or sell the goods of any soldier while he is in camp." Upon this, all the *nexi* there enroll for service (*qui aderant nexi profiteri extemplo nomina*), and the others, learning that their creditors no longer have the right to hold them captive (*retinendi ius creditori non esse*), run to the forum to take the military oath (*ut sacramento dicerent*). Livy adds that these *nexi* formed a considerable military body, the very corps that eclipsed all others in the ensuing war, both in its courage and its deeds (*magna ea manus fuit; neque aliorum magis in Volsco bello virtus atque opera enituit*).

Historians are free to think that what they have here is pure history; in other words, a real, accidental event, recorded and embellished by "tradition." I think that it is epic in nature, which is to say – in the sense made clear earlier – it is Roman mythology. Not that the two conceptions are mutually exclusive, of course, since myth is often no more than the transposition into a typical and unique narrative (presented as a fable, or lent verisimilitude according to the taste of the narrator) of a regular mechanism or behavior of a particular society. It is not impossible that, in very early Roman times, a mechanism existed that enabled victims of the *nexum* to free themselves, on a more or less regular basis – not "in return for *virtus*" but rather "in order to display *virtus*"; not "by redeeming themselves" through their exploits but by truly canceling their past, by beginning a new kind of life. Livy (or the annalists who preceded him) would then have been simply summing up in a single event, presented as fortuitous, old traditions relating to this obsolete custom. But, in any case, that could be no more than a hypothesis. The only factual datum is the epic story, which is enough for those exploring Roman sociology. It expresses, in classical costume, the opposition between the automatic and blind law of the jurist and the flexible counter-law of the warrior. In opposition to a capitalist morality based upon magico-religious sovereignty, it erects a heroic mystique that has as its justification the shifting, unpredictable task of the *milites.* For the mechanism geared to function *per aes et libram*, it substitutes an entirely heterogeneous commitment – the *sacramentum*, made man to man, in front of the commander-in-chief. Once stripped of the "legionary" form that it has acquired in Livy, this band of former *nexi*, which distinguishes itself by courage and deeds (*virtute* and *opera*) in the legendary war that Rome saw as the origin of its empire, is doubtless one of the rare pieces of evidence we have relating to the very earliest Italian *Männerbünde.*[5]

Chapter VII

*Wôdhanaz and *Tîwaz

Collaboration Between Antithetical Sovereign Gods

It is now time to confront the systems already investigated with the homologous systems found among other peoples speaking Indo-European languages. Before that, however, I shall set out clearly the constants and variables encountered so far.

Thus far, both in Rome and among the Indo-Iranians, we have brought together various pairings or "couples" – of notions, of human or divine personages, of ritual, political or legal activities, of naturalist symbols – that are everywhere apprehended as antithetical. This characteristic could develop, theoretically, in two directions. To say "antithetical" is to say either "opposed" or "complementary"; the antithesis could be expressed either by conflict or by collaboration. In practice, however, we have nowhere encountered conflict, but rather, in all areas and in a variety of forms, collaboration.

There is no trace of conflict, either mythic or ritual, between Mitra and Varuṇa, or rather, to give them their dual form, within Mitrāvaruṇā. Neither is there conflict between Mithra and Ahura-Mazdāh, even though a jealously "Mazdean" Iran had every reason to isolate its great god and abase before him everything that was not of him. The *Gāthās* make no mention of Mithra, and do not make him into a *daēva*. Then, as soon as he reappears and everywhere that he reappears, he is the "almost equal" and distinguished collaborator of Ahura-Mazdāh.

In Rome, it does not matter at all that Numa's views are diametrically opposed to those of Romulus: "history" still takes the greatest pains to avoid even the shadow of a conflict between them. They meet neither in time nor space, even though their lives slightly overlapped. Typologically, Numa, even when reforming or actually annulling his predecessor's work, is thought of as "completing" or "perfecting" it, not abolishing it. The work of Romulus subsists after Numa, and throughout its long existence Rome will be able to call upon both its fathers equally. Ritually, the Luperci and the flamen dialis (and no doubt the flamines in general) are certainly opposites in every way as regards their behavior, yet the opposition remains morphological: on the one day of the year when the Luperci get wild they do not find their "foils" standing in their way. On the contrary, on the morning of the Lupercalia, the flamen dialis, his wife, the rex, and the pontifices appear to accord the wild magicians both an investiture and a free hand.

Whenever such a couple – or one of its two components, thereby explicitly or implicitly involving the other – finds itself engaged in a conflict, its adversary is always external, heterogeneous, as in the conflict we have just observed between Indra and Varuṇa, or that between the *sacramentum* and the *nexum*.

In particular, neither in Rome nor in India nor Iran do our couples appear in certain mythic and ritual episodes to which their antithetical structure might be thought to make them specifically suited. I am referring to the various narratives and scenarios of "temporary kingship" ("false king," "carnival king," etc.). Such stories are encountered in India, with the overweening Nahuṣa thrusting himself between the fall and restoration of Indra; in Iran, with the monstrous tyrant Asdahāk seizing power between the fall of Yim and the advent of Faridūn; and in Rome, in the legends that serve as myth for the annual *regifugium*, with Tarquinius Superbus taking power between Servius Tullius and the consulate. In every case, we are dealing with a "bad" or "wicked" king, a temporary usurper, framed between two legitimate, "good" reigns. Also in every case, as can easily be verified, at least one of the two legitimate rulers, either the one before usurpation or the one after, and sometimes both (Indra-Indra; Faridūn; the consul Brutus) is or are of the *military*, a combatant. These two features radically distinguish such stories from those in which our couples appear. First, both components of the Varuṇa-Mitra couple, as well as of the Romulus-Numa couple, are equally legitimate, equally necessary, equally worthy of imitation, and equally "good" in the broad sense of the word. (In particular, as we have seen, "terrible" kings, even when they come to a bad end, are not "bad" kings.) Second, although Roman positivism has tended to reduce Romulus to a strictly warrior-type, all four are something quite different from "military leaders": Varuṇa and Mitra, Romulus and Numa are all kings in their essence, one pair by virtue of their creative violence, the other by virtue of their organizing wisdom.[1]

The Priority of the Terrible Sovereign

Within these couples, when they are constituted by human or divine personages, it has been possible to observe a kind of supremacy of one of the two components – and always the same one. This supremacy is difficult to formulate, and of no great consequence; it is usually external and quantitative rather than qualitative; but it is a fact too constant to be passed over in silence.

Mitra is a very pale figure among the Indians of Vedic times, even though – possibly merely for reasons of rhythm – he figures first in the ordinary term for the couple (Mitrāvaruṇā or, simply, Mitrā, in the dual; cf. Avestic Mithra-Ahura). He has only a single hymn that is specifically his in the *Ṛg Veda*; everywhere else he appears within the surroundings of Varuṇa, who is, on the contrary, very strongly characterized and has a great many hymns to himself. Varuṇa very often represents the couple entirely on his own (guaranteeing justice, annexing the day as well as the night to himself), whereas such an expansion would be exceptional, if it could be found, on the part of Mitra. When a reformed Iran isolated a single sovereign god and set him over the entire universe, it was Ahura, not Mithra, who benefited from this promotion. In Rome, on the divine level, it was Jupiter who captured Dius Fidius, and who became, when there is no call for fine distinctions, the god of both day-lightning and night-lightning, as well as the god of the oath, of Fides itself. On the human level, Romulus is the true founder of Rome, while Numa, historically, is only the second, his second.

Reasonably convincing explanations can be put forth for this particular form of relation. Since these personages fall into the categories, among others, of magician-creator and jurist-organizer, it is quite obvious that they are bound to "succeed" one another, at the beginning of a world or at least a state, cosmogonically or historically, in accordance with an inevitable order Ahura-Mazdāh creates, Romulus founds, but Mithra and Numa cannot organize and regulate until that has been done. Moreover, since our earliest Indian documentary evidence consists of texts relating to sacrifice, to the magico-religious life, and not juridical or economic texts, it is natural that of the two sovereigns it should be Varuṇa, not Mitra, who is predominant. These considerations, one must admit, are certainly rational enough; but in our field of study it is necessary to be wary of "proofs by reason." Let us simply say, for the time being, that the couples expressing the Roman and Indo-Iranian conceptions of sovereignty present themselves with a *de facto* hierarchy that does not exclude a *de jure* equality. A further element, to be introduced shortly, will enable us to clarify this situation somewhat, if not to interpret it.

Mithra Armed

Having listed these agreements, we must now take note of a difference, one that is all the more interesting because it leaves Vedic India isolated in the face of Rome and Iran: the Avestic Mithra *also* presents himself as an armed god, a combatant. His entire *Yast* depicts him as embattled, and he is closely associated with Vṛthragna, the spirit of offensive victory. In Vedic India, on the contrary, Indra, and Indra alone, is the god who strikes like the thunderbolt, while Mitra never engages in combat in any form; and, again, it was Indra who was linked so early and so closely with Vṛtrahan that he absorbed him, and became for the cycles of the ages "Indra-Vṛtrahan." One detail expresses this difference in a very tangible way. The Indo-Iranians already possessed a name for and a precise representation of the divine weapon: the Sanskrit *vajra*, the Avestic *vazra* (whence by borrowing, in the Finno-Ugric languages, come the Finnish *vasara* and Lapp *vaecer* for "hammer," and the Mordvin *vizir* for "axe": Setälä, *Finn.-ugr Forschungen*, VIII, 1908, pp. 79-80). And M.B. Geiger (*Sitzb. d. Ak. d. Wiss.*, Wien, 1916, 176, 7, p. 74ff.) has pointed out coincidences in the Indian and Iranian descriptions of these two weapons which in fact seem to guarantee a prehistoric figuration and even prehistoric formulas. Now, the *vajra* (Donnerkeil, thunderbolt-weapon) is exclusive to Indra, while the *vazra* is exclusively the "club" of Mithra.

It is probable that this Iranian state of things is the result of an evolution. In the first place, it must fall within the intentions of the Zoroastrian reformers who extended their moral system even to the field of war, as well as to the particular form of relations there between warrior power and the royal administration. Whereas in ancient India, a land of many small kingdoms, the fighter Vṛtrahan (or, more precisely, Indra-Vṛtrahan) became highly developed and quickly pushed Mitra and Varuṇa, along with the Āditya as a whole, into the background (of the whole of post-Vedic religion). In imperial Iran, on the contrary, Vṛthragna remained the genie, the "officer" of a precise function – offensive victory – while the essential role of state religion became fixed on the truly sovereign entities: Ahura-Mazdāh, with his council of abstract powers, and also Mithra. And it is Mithra, in those sections of the Avesta where he is accepted, who has annexed the various traits of the warrior-god, without going quite so far, nevertheless, as to absorb Vṛthragna. Whatever the details of these developments, that at least is their probable direction.

However, it is also possible that the Iranian Mithra, a fighter armed with the *vazra*, simply developed a power already inherent in the Indo-Iranian **Mitra*, one that the Vedic Mitra let fall into disuse. Although, in Rome, neither Numa, Fides nor Dius Fidius is in any degree a fighter, Dius Fidius, in his role as jurist, a thunderbolt god, is nevertheless armed with the *fulmen* he employs to "sanction" the *faedera*, as his other name (Semo Sancus) seems to indicate, and as Virgil tells us when he transfers the term to the Jupiter complex (*Aeneid*, XII, 200). It is the thunderbolt of a notary, not that of a captain – a legal impress rather than a weapon of war, but a thunderbolt all the same. It is also worth noting that the terrible Jupiter, the other component of the Roman sovereign couple, is also – in essence and in a warlike context – a god of lightning. It is he (as Elicius) who presents the good and peace-loving Numa with the awesome problem of how to ward off his lightning – the problem, that is, of human sacrifice. And Mars, the Roman god of the *milites*, whose cosmic domain is in fact the lower atmosphere and the earth's surface – Mars, the god of battle, is not a wielder of the thunderbolt.[2] In that respect, too, Rome is in conflict with India and in agreement with Iran, whose victorious genie Vṛthragna is also not armed with lightning. India, on the contrary, is in agreement here with the Germanic world, where the god of the second of the three cosmic and social functions, the fighter-champion, is called Thor, which is to say **Thunraz* or "Thunder," and is armed with a hammer that is also a thunderbolt.

Uranos and Zeus

One might think that the perspectives opened up by this book regarding the early Indo-European conception of sovereignty ought to enable me to complete the short book I devoted to *Ouranos-Varuṇa* in 1934, in which Mitra was neglected. In fact, however, they merely shed further light on the peculiarity of the Greek myths, and the impossibility of reducing them to the Indo-European systems.[3]

Uranos does not form a couple with any other god. Beside this terrible king, this binder with his irresistible powers of seizure, this chaotic creator, we find no ordered, lawgiving, organizing sovereign on his "mythic level." It is true that such a sovereign does appear later in the story – Zeus. But he does not come as one part of a couple to balance Uranos, not even in the same way as Numa balances Romulus; instead, he comes to abolish his predecessor's mode of activity forever, to begin a new phase in the world's life – one in which the powerful whim of Uranos will no longer have a place, either as driving force, model or object of worship. So in what measure are this Zeus and this Uranos – the one the luminous sky and the other the night sky, the one a warrior with his thunderbolt and the other a "seizing and binding" magician, the one *δικαῖος* (even though Prometheus would disagree) and the other chaotic, the one merely superhuman and the other monstrous – in what measure are they heirs, within a quite different theological framework, of the ancient, balanced couple whose Indo-European antiquity is so amply underwritten by the Roman and Indo-Iranian evidence? In his defeat Uranos was hurled into the dark reaches of fabulous times, and thus, as it were, beyond us whereas Zeus lives on with us, among us. Is this difference of "framework" equivalent in some way to what the Indians mean when they say that "Mitra is this world, Varuṇa is the other world"? It would not be the first time that relations in space had evolved and had been reformulated into relations in time.

We are assured, however, that Zeus and the living religious concepts of Greece in their entirety are essentially formed of a substance that is Aegean and not Indo-European. What to me seemed to have come from the Indo-European fund can no longer be regarded as more than fable, matter for literature alone, not for worship. Here Uranos, there the centaurs; but no, those "everyday" monsters, embodied in processions, are not the centaurs, only satyrs and silens; and Uranos is now nothing more than the figurehead of an "academic" cosmogony. We must not therefore search for any simple relation between the fossil Uranos and the living Zeus. Above all, we must not suppose too hastily that Zeus could have acquired, like Mithra in Iran, a warlike appearance and a lawyer's soul. The object of my present investigation no longer has any existence in Greece, since no form of Greek mythology or society is any longer articulated by the Indo-European schema of the "three social functions (or classes)" that were preserved in India, in Iran and in very early Rome, and that are still recognizable in the Celtic and Germanic worlds.[4] Zeus does indeed preside over a divine hierarchy, but of a different type, probably Aegean, in which Poseidon and the waters of the sea, Pluto and the underworld, are the other components. It is true that in every area of Greece war and agriculture have their patron figures; but nowhere beneath the magic sovereign do they form that triad, of which the three flamines, Jupiter, Mars and Quirinus, riding in the same chariot to sacrifice to Fides Publica, are still such clear-cut evidence. Perhaps a time will come when we will be able to make a probable distinction regarding, not only the relations of Uranos and Zeus, but also those of Uranos and Oceanos and of both with Kronos, between the Aegean data and the shreds of Indo-European material that have successfully survived around the names of the personages (which are either certainly or probably Indo-European). But for the present I shall pass by the temples of Greece without entering – consigned punishment, perhaps, for having explored them without sufficient prudence in my earliest forays.

There will be occasion, moreover, to extend the inquiry beyond the Uranides later. One of my students, Lucien Gerschel, is now investigating the problem of how far the oppositions defined in this book can be linked to the opposition, so dear to Nietzsche and so perfectly real, between Apollo and Dionysos.

***Wôdhanaz and *Tîwaz**

In a recent work (*Mythes et dieux des Germains*, 1939, ch. 1: "Mythologie indo-européenne et mythologie germanique"), I began the task of comparing the earliest forms of religious representation in the Indo-European North with the system that emerges from a comparison of East and West, that is, from the Indo-Iranian, Italic and Celtic data. At that time I commented on the way the absence of a large priestly body, analogous to the brahmans, the magi, the Druids or the pontifical college (flamines and pontiffs), in combination with the ideal of a classless society (which had struck Caesar so forcibly among the peoples beyond the Rhine), had softened the system without actually dismantling it. We can still recognize, in various formulas, in divine groupings, in the general division of the mythology, that great triple division of cosmic and social functions: magical sovereignty (and heavenly administration of the universe), warrior power (and administration of the lower atmosphere), peaceful fecundity (and administration of the earth, the underworld and the sea). The Scandinavian triad is defined in precisely this way: Odhinn, the sovereign magician; Thor, the champion-thunderer; Freyr (or Njödhr), lubricious and peaceful producer. Possibly, these are the triad already recorded by a disconcerted Caesar in excessively naturalist terms: Sol, Vulcanus, Luna; in other words, we may assume, *Tîwaz or *Wôdhanaz, *Thunraz, *Nerthuz (*De Bello Gallico*, VI, 21; cf. my *Mythes et dieux*..., p. 12); and also the triad discernible in Tacitus (*Germania*, 2), behind the religious groups descended from the mythical sons of Mannus, Erminones, Istraeones (a better reading than Istuaevones), Inguaeones (*Ermenaz: cf. Old Scand. *jörmunr*, appellation of Odhinn; *Istraz: adjective in **-raz* from IE **-ro-*, a frequent formation in the names of powerful fighting gods: Indra, Rudra, *Thunraz himself; *Inguaz: cf. Old Scand. Yngvi, appellation of Freyr; see J. de Vries, *Altgermanische Religionsgeschicte*, I, 1935, pp. 212-216).

But among the Germanic peoples, as in Rome and in the Indo-Iranian world, the first function, sovereignty, is not presided over by a single god. In Scandinavia, beside Odhinn there is Ullr (Norway, north and central Sweden) or Tyr (Denmark, Scania). On the continent, alongside *Wôdhanaz there is *Tîwaz or *Tiuz (German Wotan and Ziu). When Tacitus (*Germania*, 9) names the three great gods of the German tribes as Mercurius, Mars and Hercules, we should recognize them as the couple *Wôdhanaz-*Tîwaz, the two gods of sovereignty, plus the champion *Thunraz (J. de Vries, *Altgerm. Religionsgesch.*, I, pp. 166-179). The patron of agriculture, whoever he was, is omitted, probably because of the contempt in which he was held, at least in theory, as noted by Caesar earlier (*agriculturae non student*, etc.; *De Bell. Gall.*, VI, 22). Tacitus goes on to say that the god he has called Mercurius requires human victims on a particular day, whereas Mars and Hercules require only animal sacrifices: an excellent criterion that defines one of the two sovereigns as "terrible" in contrast both to the other sovereign and to the warrior god; and this fits nicely with the Indian and Roman sets of data dealt with in preceding chapters.

In Chapter 2 of *Mythes et dieux des Germains*, I examined the narratives of Saxo Grammaticus, which, opposing as they do Othinus and Ollerus (that is, Odhinn and Ullr) or Othinus and Mithothyn (that is, Odhinn and *mjötudh-inn*, "the judge-leader" or, less probably, "the anti-Odhinn"), enable us to define each of the components of these couples in relation to the other. Let me stress first, however, that contrary to what we have constantly found in Rome, Iran and

India, the mythological theme of the "bad, temporary king" is fused with the mythological theme of the "two antithetical types of sovereign": Ollerus and Mithothyn are both usurpers who occupy the sovereign's place only during Othinus's absences (either obligatory or voluntary) from power. Here, I shall leave the "Othinus-Ollerus" form of the antithesis to one side. It does in fact open up a very important line of research, but one that we cannot pursue here, since Ullr seems to be opposed to Odhinn, his other specifications apart, as the patron of very specific techniques (he is the "inventor" of the skate, the ski, etc.), in contrast to Odhinn's all-powerful magic – an artisan god as opposed to a shaman god. And it will not suffice, in this context, merely to liken him to the Irish *Lug samildânach*, "the god of all trades," the artisan god to whom the king-god in a well-known mythological story (*La Seconde Bataille de Mag Tured, Revue Celtique*, XII, 1891, section 74), voluntarily gives up his throne for thirteen days, since it is the entire question of "craft religions" that would have to be investigated throughout the entire Indo-European world, which, in turn, would entail a consideration of the concordance, and sometimes the union, of the concepts of jurist and artisan, law and recipe, legal practice and technical craft. For the moment, then, let me simply repeat that, from their names alone, Ullr (also called Ullinn, a form well attested by Norwegian toponymy: Magnus Olsen, *Hedenske Kultminder i norske Stedsnavne*, I, Oslo, 1915, p. 104ff.) and Odhinn (derived from *ôdhr*, which, moreover, exists as the name of a god) coincide very closely indeed with the opposition we have been exploring in earlier chapters: Ullr, a Scandinavian form of the Gothic *wulthus*, "*δόξα*," expresses "majestic glory,"[5] while *ôdhr*, the Scandinavian form of German *Wut* and Gothic *woths* "*δαιμονιζόμενος*," denotes all the material and moral forms of frenetic agitation (J. de Vries, *Folklore Fellows Communications*, 94, Helsinki, 1931, p. 31: "rapid and wild motions of sea, fire, storm" and also "drunkenness, excitation, poetic frenzy"; as an adjective, *ôdhr* is to be translated either as "terrible, furious" or as "rapid, swift"); and I can only refer readers to what was said earlier, with reference to homologous beings, about the mystique of *celeritas*. De Vries, whose vegetation theory for Odhinn I do not entirely accept, nevertheless gives very good definitions of the etymology of the two gods: Ullin-Ullr is "a divine person whose activity consists in a cosmic brilliance"; Odhinn is the possessor of the multiform *ôdhr*, of that night-favoring *Wut* that also animates, on the continent, those wild rides in the supernatural hunt, *das wütende Heer*, of which Wôde or Wôden is sometimes still the leader, just as the terrible *Harii* warriors, with their black shields and painted bodies, chose the darkest nights for combat and gave themselves the appearance of a *feralis exercitus* (Tacitus, *Germania*, 43; cf. the *ein-herjar*, that is, **aina-hariya-*, dead warriors who form Odhinn's court in the other world). It is gratifying to find the same symbolic opposition coloring these two northern figures of sovereignty, the same contrast between light and darkness we have already observed, in varying forms, in India (Mitra, day: Varuṇa, night) and in Rome (Jupiter, "Summanus": Dius Fidius, "diurnus"). In the *Wôdhanaz-*Tîwaz form of the couple, the same nuance is again attested by the etymology of the second name: *Tîwaz is IE **deiwo-*, Sanskrit *devạh*, Latin *deus* – in other words, a god whose essence contains the light of heaven.

However, it is in his role as jurist that the adversary of Othinus will prove of particular interest to us here.

Chapter VIII

"Communiter" and "Discreta Cuique"

**Tîwaz: War and the Law*[1]

In my research Jan de Vries has aided me greatly with his passages devoted to the Germanic god Romanized as Mars. This god must certainly be *Tîwaz, homonym of the Scandinavian Tyr (*Altgerm. Religionsgesch.*, I, pp. 170-175). *Tîwaz undoubtedly had an essential connection with military activity, since both the local population and Romans sensed his resemblance to Mars. Yet one could and should say the same for the majority of the Germanic gods. Julius Caesar was very emphatic that the only activities in which the continental Germanic tribes deigned to take an interest were war and preparation for war; nothing else counted. And I, too, have noted this "military inclination" in the entire mythology, beginning with Odhinn himself (*Mythes et dieux*..., p. 145ff.). However, to content ourselves with affixing such a summary label is scarcely permissible.

What are the relations of *Tîwaz-Mars to war? To begin with, relations that are not exclusive, as he has other activities. In several inscriptions he is qualified as Thincsus, which means, despite interminable arguments on the matter, that he is, without a doubt, protector of the *thing* (German *Ding*) – in other words, of the people when assembled in a body to arrive at judgments and to make decisions. But even apart from this important civil function, *Tîwaz-Mars remains a jurist in war itself. And here let me quote de Vries (*op. cit.*, pp. 173-175): "Thus the god Mars Thincsus was closely connected with the people's assembly, with the *Ding*; the same thing can be seen in Denmark, where *Tislund*, in Zealand, was a place of assembly. *Tîwaz was therefore both a protector in battle and a protector of the assembly. In general, his character as a god of war has been brought too much into the foreground, and his significance for Germanic law insufficiently recognized.... These two conceptions (god of battles, god of law) are not contradictory. War is not, in fact, the bloody hand-to-hand combat of battle; it is a *decision*, arrived at by combat between two parties, and governed by precise rules in law. One has only to read in the works of historians how the Germans were already fixing the time and the place of their encounters with the Romans to realize that for them a battle was an action to be carried out in accordance with fixed legal rules. Expressions such as *Schwertding*, or Old Scandinavian *vâpnadômr*, are not poetic figures, but correspond precisely to ancient practice. The symbolic gestures linked with combat are incontestable proofs of this: the declaration of war among the Latins by the *hasta ferrata aut praeusta sanguinea* is directly comparable to the ceremony in which the northern Germans hurled a spear at an opposing army. And that spear bears the same essential significance as the one planted at the center of the *Ding*: if the Scandinavian Tyr bore a spear, as J. Grimm has already pointed out, it was less as a weapon than as a sign of juridical power (cf. H. Meyer, *Heerfahne und Rolandsbild, Nachr. d. Gesellsch. f. Wiss., Ph.-hist. Klasse*, Göttingen, 1930, p. 460ff.). From these facts considered as a whole, it becomes evident that, in every respect, the name Mars Thincsus is a very fitting one for this god of law. Naturally, the Romans were unable to perceive him as anything more than a god of war because their first contacts with the German tribes were all in terms of war."

That is an excellent summary which makes plain that the sociological mythology of our day is no more satisfied with summary definitions such as "military god," "agricultural god," than with those other definitions that were once regarded as exhaustive, such as "sun god," "storm spirit" or "vegetation spirit." There are many ways of being a war god, and *Tîwaz is a clear example of one very poorly defined by such labels as "warrior god" or "god of battle." The legitimate patron of battle (defined as an exchange of blows) is *Thunraz, the champion (cf. *Mythes et dieux*..., ch. VII), the model of physical force, the divinity whose name the Romans translated as Hercules. *Tîwaz is something quite different: the jurist of war and, at the same time, a kind of diplomat, rather like those *fetiales* supposedly created by the peace-loving legislator Numa (or by his grandson and imitator Ancus) in order to reduce or curb violence. As for *Wôdhanaz, he is not a fighter either – any more than the binder Varuṇa is; even in battle, he remains the magician.[2] Patron of the band of men-beasts, the *Berserkir* or the *Ulfhedhnir*, the "bear-coats" or "wolf-skins" (as Varuṇa is of the half-man, half-horse Gandharva, as Romulus is of the feral band of Luperci), *Wôdhanaz communicates his own gifts to them: the power of metamorphosis, *furor* (*ôdhr*!), invulnerability, certainty of aim and, above all, a paralyzing power by which the enemy is immobilized, blinded, deafened, disarmed and brought to its knees before it has even begun to fight. In one famous story (*Saga des Völsungar*, XI, end), we see him rise up in the very heart of the battle, one-eyed, fate-bearing, brandishing a spear that he does not use to fight with but against which the sword of the chief, whose death he has decreed, is shattered; and, abruptly, the tide of battle turns: those about to conquer weaken, then fall as one, and are conquered. It is precisely the technique of Jupiter Stator, of that terrible sovereign homologous with Odhinn – a technique of an omnipotent wizard, not that of a fighting warrior. Moreover, according to Ranisch (*Eddalieder*, Göschen Collection, no. 171,

p. 111n.), the early Scandinavians called this paralyzing fear, this military panic, *herfjöturr*, "army bond" or "army shackle." It will come as no surprise to the reader to find the image of the "bond" appearing at this point; and I shall take advantage of this opportunity to take sides in the argument relating to an apposite passage in Tacitus (*Germania*, 39; cf. J. de Vries, *Altgerm. Religionsgesch.*, I, pp. 180-181).[3] Among the Semnones, the *regnator omnium deus* has a sacred wood, and not only are human sacrifices made there, but no one may set foot within it *nisi vinculo ligatus*, "unless bound with a shackle" – precisely, says Tacitus, to indicate that the place belongs to that *regnator* to whom everything and everyone else owes obedience, *cetera subiecta atque parentia*. In which case, it certainly cannot be the jurist sovereign who is involved, but rather the terrible sovereign, not *Tîwaz but *Wôdhanaz. This whole present comparative inquiry confirms the indication of such an identification already provided by the link between Odhinn and the *Fjöturlundr*, the "sacred wood of the Bond," in *Helgakvidha Hundingsbana* II (prose before strophe 38), and renders null and void the frail arguments to the contrary with which all the writers in the field seem to have been satisfied hitherto, with the exceptions of K. Zeuss, A. Baumstark, G. Neckel, B. Kummer and Jan de Vries.[4]

Saxo, I, 7 and Caesar, VI, 22

But let us return to times of peace. The legend that opposes Othinus and Mithothyn (Saxo Grammaticus, I, 7) raises a difficulty of great importance. Let me begin by summarizing the story. His kingly dignity having been sullied by the misconduct of his wife, Othinus goes into voluntary exile. In his absence, a magician, Mithothyn, usurps his place and introduces an essential change into the mode of worship: "He asserted that the anger and resentment of the gods could not be appeased by conjoined and mingled sacrifices; he therefore forbade them to offer up their prayers collectively, establishing separate libations for each of the gods" (*Hic deorum iram aut numinum violationem* confusis permixtisque sacrificiis *expiari negabat; ideoque eis vota* communiter *nuncupari prohibebat,* discreta superum cuique libamenta constituens). But Othinus abruptly reappears, and the usurper flees and meets a wretched end, whereupon the legitimate king reestablishes the previous order, "obliging all those who had borne the titles of celestial honors in his absence to lay them down, as not rightfully theirs" (*Cunctos qui per absentiam suam caelestium honorum titulos gesserant tanquam alienos* deponere coegit).

Thus the usurper, the one of the pair who is the "bad" king, fleeting as opposed to durable, is not the "inspired madman"; he is the "distributor," he is not the god of tumult (*Odhinn-ôdhr*); he is the judge-leader (*mjötudhinn*), in other words, a personage of the *Tîwaz type. A scandal, no less! If we transfer this legend, undoubtedly an ancient myth, into human reality, we are forced to envisage a society whose entire life consists of one vast Lupercalia interrupted by a single brief period every year in which life is regulated by law; in other words, the exact opposite of what we found in Rome, for example, and recognized as being in conformity with reason.

Once again, however, let us be wary of reason. And first of all, let us take care not to confuse the representations a society creates from its own mechanisms with the actual functioning of those mechanisms in reality. It is quite true that mythologies project into the "Great World" the machinery of this one; but the "Great World" can tolerate anything; there, there is no need for the compromises, for the hypocrisies that, in this low world of ours, enable the majority of societies to live without too great a strain, proclaiming an ideal while betraying it at every moment. That is true in our modern world, and it was true among the ancient Germans. Saxo's legend, or rather the ancient myth to which it bears witness, does not prove that the users or consumers of that myth lived a life that ran diametrically counter to our own good sense; but perhaps it does prove that it would have been their ideal to lead such a life, and that they pretended to live it. A passage from Caesar's *De Bello Gallico* (VI, 22) enables us to be rather more positive in this matter, since in this case it does not define a myth, but a feature of early Germanic economic ethics that is again "excessive," that again corresponds to an ideal rather than to practice, and of which the underlying principle is the same as that which triumphs in the passage from Saxo.

"No man," Caesar tells us, writing of the German tribes, "has any fixed quantity of land, or sites that belong specifically to him. Each year the magistrates and chiefs parcel out the land among the *gentes* and among groups of kinfolk living communally, in such quantities and in such places as they deem fitting. The following year they oblige them to move elsewhere" (neque quisquam agri modum certum aut fines habet proprios; *sed magistratus ac principes* in annos singulos *gentibus cognationibusque hominum qui una coierunt quantum et quo loco visum est agri distribuunt, atque* anno post alio transire cogunt). And Caesar then records as many as five justifications for this system, all of them, he assures us, provided by those involved (*eius rei multas afferunt causas*). Moreover, all five justifications are admirable ones, and for our purposes have the advantage of providing proof that there actually is an economic mystique involved here, an ideal of purity and justice that could thus be maintained and loudly proclaimed as an ideal even at a time when practice was already perceptibly diverging from it; for I accept entirely, along with the legal historians, that even at the time of Caesar and Tacitus (a parallel but obscure passage in *Germania*, 26), there already existed among the Germans *festes und geregeltes Grundeigentum* (J. Grimm, *Deutsche Rechtsaltertümer*, II, 1899, p. 7n.). Thus these five *causas* (or "reasons") lie in the moral domain: Caesar tells us that the Germans feared that prolonged habituation to agriculture would cause them to lose the taste for war; to yield to peasant greed, with the injustices that brings in its wake; to become demanding in the matter of comfort; to see factions and discords arising among them caused by love of wealth; and, lastly – a positive argument – that their communizing system was well suited to satisfying and containing the people, "since each member...can see that his resources are equal to those of the most powerful" (*ut animi aequitate plebem contineant, quum suas quisque opes cum potentissimis aequari videat*).

Totalitarian and Distributive Economies

I have emphasized in these two texts, that from Saxo and that from Caesar, the terms that correspond. In Saxo, Mithothyn's error is to condemn "the good system," that is, the *confusa permixtaque sacrificia*, the offerings made to all members of divine society *communiter*, and to institute *discreta superum cuique libamenta*. But when Othinus returns, as representative of "the good system," he forthwith strips these pseudo-proprietors of their titles, forces them to lay those usurped honors down (*tanquam alienos deponere coegit*), and, though the text does not explicitly say so, clearly reestablishes the old system. In Caesar, "the good system" consists in preventing any person from establishing any true ownership, *neque quiquam agri modum certum aut fines habet proprios.* Once a year, of necessity (because the land must be cultivated), temporary distribution (*distribuunt*) of the land is made among the members of society; but, also once a year, the leaders force those pseudo-proprietors to abandon the lands consigned to them (*alio transire cogunt*). In the one instance, divine society alone is involved, and the only properties in question are the benefits, the sacrifices, conferred by worship; in the other, human society is involved, and the properties are areas of land. But the principle is the same: the same consecration of a communizing system, the same repugnance for permanent enclosure and appropriation.

There is no means of establishing, or, indeed, any necessity to think, that the prehistoric myth from which the Scandinavian legend derived was in fact the very myth that corresponded to an annual practice ensuring that collective wealth, temporarily divided and owned, was recalled and merged once more into that ideal "unity." But it is more than probable that the annual mechanism described by Caesar, even though much attenuated and almost obsolete, was backed up by mythical representations. Moreover, those representations could not have been very different from Saxo's narrative, and, since a function of the sovereigns was involved (Caesar writes: *magistratus* ac principes *distribuunt... cogunt*), the two gods symbolizing the two rival structures must have been, as in Saxo's story, the two sovereign gods: the jurist-god and the inspired-god, *Tîwaz and *Wôdhanaz. The condemnation of the "stable and liberal economy" presided over by *Tîwaz was a preparation for the glorification of the "shifting and totalitarian economy" presided over by *Wôdhanaz.

This text of Saxo's therefore obliges us to introduce a new and all-important consideration into the theory of sovereignty: that of the *economic system* within which, along with the two sovereign gods, the coupled concepts, rituals and moralities they represent are seen to function. This fact has not become evident before because India, Iran and Rome have all presented us with societies that are equivalent in this respect, since all have systems of divided, stable and hereditary property. In their case, the wealth of each person, or at least of each autonomous group (of the *gens*, for example), is fundamental and sacred. And all types of relations, even those between man and god and god and man, are conceived of in accordance with one and the same model: the ceding of property with precisely specified compensation. The ideal of such societies is a division of wealth kept as strict and as clear as possible, with a view to peaceful enjoyment of it. A day of undefined violence, like that erupting in the Lupercalia, can be no more than an exception during the year, as feared as it is necessary. The everyday, permanent morality is that of the flamines.

In contrast, the ideal of the early Germanic societies, as recorded by Caesar, is a "confusionism," a permanent social melting-pot, a "unanism" upholding a heroic and anti-capitalist ethic. Each year, during a single and doubtless brief meeting, this confusionism is given its full realization as the wealth temporarily distributed the previous year is returned to the community. That wealth is then immediately redistributed for the next period; nonetheless, this distribution is apprehended as an evil, a lesser evil, that the Germans would have liked to avoid. Their mystique of *aequitas*, as Caesar terms it (an equality secured by the negation of property so as to maintain a warlike *Stimmung*), must cause them to regard that annual day or group of days as an exception as regrettable as it is necessary, devoted as it is to organizing a system in violation of their ideal that, however uncertain and temporary, constitutes a minimum of ownership and a risk or an onset of appropriation.

The opposition is thus total. And yet perhaps India, Iran and Rome do bear in their very mythology the mark of a prehistoric system comparable to that of the Germans. We know how very conservative myths, and the legends in which they survive, can sometimes be. For instance, the passage from Saxo we are dealing with now is remarkable not only as regards its "morality," but also as regards the contradiction that exists, as far back as we can reach in history, between that morality and Scandinavian practice. If there is one area of the Germanic world in which hereditary property and family wealth acquired "sacred" value and functions very early on, that area is Scandinavia (cf. Magnus Olsen, *Ättegaard og Helligdom*, Oslo, 1926). That being so, are we not justified in perceiving an archaism of the same kind in the anomaly I indicated earlier without attempting to explain it? To wit, in Rome as in India, the predominant god of the divine sovereign couple is not the ordered, just god (Dius Fidius, Mitra), but on the contrary the terrible, magician god (Jupiter, Varuṇa), even though the fundamental religion is, in practice, that of the flamines and the *brahmans*, not that of the Luperci and the Gandharva?

At all events, the information on the Germanic world provided by these passages from Caesar and Saxo enables us to gauge, in one precisely defined context, the irreparable loss for the comparatist created by the almost total disappearance of the Slavonic mythologies; for a few names of gods with brief definitions cannot, in effect, be called a mythology. Yet forms of collective ownership with periodic redistribution of wealth are known to have existed among the Slavs even into the historic era. Their mythology of sovereignty must have been modeled on these practices; and it would have been all the more interesting to have known what precise form it took, for the human depositories of sovereignty among the Slavs appear to have been more than commonly unstable. But all that is irremediably lost.

Nuada and Bress

I said earlier that Saxo's text dealing with the "temporary usurpations" of Mithothyn and Ollerus show that the Germans, unlike the Indo-Iranians and the Romans, fused into a single schema the two mythical themes of the two "good" sovereign gods as antithetical couple and of the "bad" temporary sovereign. This gives us good reason to look at related mythologies with a view to establishing whether this second theme does not, on occasion, have an economic value there too. At first sight this appears not to be the case: the tyranny of Nahuṣa, of Aždahāk, of Tarquinius Superbus, is characterized by excessive *pride* and by serious *sexual* malefactions, demands or violent acts, rather than by economic misdeameanors. Nahauṣa demands the wife of the god-king Indra, whom he "replaces"; Aždahāk sexually possesses the two sisters of King Yim, whom he has dethroned, and Faridūn liberates them (this feature is already Avestic); Tarquin is doomed because, under his rule, under the "cover" of his kingship, he commits the greatest sexual crime in Roman fable, the rape of Lucretia. In all this, there is no economic element whatsoever, unless we take into account the links recorded by tradition between Tarquinius and forced labor (Livy, I, 56).

The economic element is, on the contrary, in the very forefront of an Irish myth that should probably be placed in this context – less for its coupled sovereign gods than for the temporary usurper it presents – and which is all the more interesting for simultaneously being – according to whichever point of view one takes – both the homologue and an inversion of the Germanic myth.

The Irish, and the sedentary Celts in general, of the period after the great migrations, are of the Roman and Indo-Iranian type with respect to property. The "confusionism" of Othinus is utterly alien to individualists, attached to wealth, and even more so to the external marks of wealth. They look on any development of central power, any control, any risk or first symptom of statism, with repugnance; and this is no doubt what is being expressed in the myth of the temporary eclipse of "Nuada of the Silver Hand," a legendary king of the Tuatha De Danann – that is, even earlier, of the gods – and himself a god whose antiquity is confirmed by the fact that he also appears in a Welsh Mabinogi under the name "Lludd of the Silver Hand" (Llud for *Nud by assonant assimilation to the initial consonant of *llaw*, "hand") and, above all, by the fact that he appears under the name Nodens, Nodons, very early in several Latin inscriptions from Great Britain. Having lost a hand, Nuada becomes unfit to reign by virtue of an ancient law common to many peoples, until such time as the physician-god and the bronzesmith-god have made him a silver replacement hand, which takes seven years. His temporary replacement is the tyrannical Bress, a chief of the Fomorians, which is to say, a being of another race that simultaneously is kin to and in fundamental conflict with the Tuatha De Danann – just as, for example, the Asura are with the Deva in India. Now, the tyranny of Bress is purely economic.[5] Greedy, and equally miserly, he demands, for the first time in history, taxes, and exorbitant taxes at that. He also introduces forced labor and declares war on private property. The ruses he employs are still famous. For example, he lays claim to the milk from all hairless, dun-colored cows. At first this bizarre specification sounds reassuring, but then he orders a great fire of ferns to be lit, and all the cows in Munster driven through it, so that their hair is singed off and their hides browned (H. d'Arbois de Jubainville, *The Irish Mythological Cycle*, trans. Richard Irvine Best, O'Donoghue & Co., Dublin, 1903). None of this wealth he extorts is used in any act of generosity, and he is eventually cursed or – which comes to the same thing – mocked by a *file*, by a poet, for his avarice. The Tuatha De Danann then oblige him to abdicate, granting him a reprieve only on one condition. You must guarantee us, under surety, they tell him, the enjoyment of all the products on which you lay your hand, houses and lands, and gold and silver and cows and victuals; and also exemption from tax (*cêis*, borrowed from Latin *census*) and fines until the end of your reign. Bress is forced to accept these conditions, but immediately goes to complain, or rather confess, to his father, asking him for help. "It is my own injustice and pride," he says, "and nothing else that have removed me [from the throne] (*nim-tucc acht m'anfhir ocus m'anuabhar fesin*). I took from my subjects their treasures and their jewels, and even their victuals; and until now no one had taxed or fined them." To this admission his father very properly replies: "It was ill done: it would have been better (to have) their (good) wishes then to reign over them; better their (good) prayers than their curses..." (*Second Battle of Mag Tured*, ed. W. Stokes, *Revue Celtique*, XII, sections 25, 40, 45, 46).

And, indeed, that is the great question, for all leaders under all skies. But one also needs to determine whether, in order to have the people's good wishes and blessings, the leader should be the active embodiment of a communizing, greedy, fiscal, dispossessing but equalizing state (which in consequence, as Caesar says of the Germans' system, *animi aequitate plebem contineat, quum suas quisquis opes cum potentissimis aequari videat*), or whether, on the contrary, he should be the figurehead of an aristocratic federation or the president of a bourgeois association, an impotent and liberal leader whose sole duty – can he but perform it – is to protect each individual against the envy of others and to guarantee him, with the minimum of taxation for public services, inviolable enjoyment of his personal wealth. It is clear that the Irish composers of this legend made the opposite choice to that of the continental German tribes observed by Caesar or of the prehistoric Scandinavians responsible for the story in Saxo. Bress and Othinus are both for state control and against private appropriation; Nuada and Mithothyn are both for personal ownership and against communism. It is just that the roles of "hero" and "villain" have been reversed: in Ireland the wicked usurper is the nationalizing Bress; in Scandinavia he is the privatizing Mithothyn.

Chapter IX

The One-Eyed God and the One-Handed God

Odhinn's Eye

Odhinn and Tyr are not just the Scandinavian heirs of the magician sovereign and the jurist sovereign. They are also the one-eyed god and the one-handed god. Their disabilities form a couple, as do their functions; and this parallelism suggests that we ought perhaps to investigate whether there is in fact any interdependence, at least on a symbolic level, between the disabilities and the functions.

Although Odhinn's one-eyed state is a constant, Jan de Vries (*Altgerm. Religionsgesch.*, II, p. 192ff.) is correct in saying that the circumstances of his mutilation are not clear. The meaning of it, however, is not inaccessible. From strophes 28 and 29 of the *Völuspâ* we know that Odhinn's lost eye is "in the spring of the Mîmir." "I know," the witch says, "I know, Odhinn, where your eye is sunk; I know that Odhinn's eye lies at the bottom of the famous spring of Mîmir (*veit hôn Odhins auga folgit î enum maera Mîmis brunni*); Mîmir drinks hydromel every morning on the pledge of the Father of warriors" (*drekr mjödh Mîmir morgon hverjan af vedhi Valfödhur*). Clearly, there is an allusion here to a story that has no other trace in the Eddic poems; but we do know who Mîmir is (J. de Vries, *op. cit.*, p. 361ff.). The name occurs in three forms denoting the possessor of three objects – the head of *Mîmr*, the tree of *Mîmi* and (just quoted) the spring of Mîmir. In all three cases, moreover, this personage is linked with the power of Odhinn. The best known of these three traditions is the one concerning the head of Mîmr, which possesses knowledge of the runes and teaches it to Odhinn. Snorri (*Ynglingasaga*, 4, at the end of his account of the war between the Ases and the Vanes) records a tradition relating to the way this head came to Odhinn's aid, and the invaluable revelations it made to him about "the hidden things." The tradition might have been embellished, but it would be incautious to reject it *in toto*. Similarly, it would be hypercritical to dismiss as pure auctorial imagination the commentary that Snorri offers on strophe 29 of the *Völuspâ* (*Gylfaginning*, 15): at the foot of one of the roots of the world-tree Mîmameidhr, there lies the spring of Mîmir (*Mîmisbrunr*), in which knowledge and intelligence lie hidden; "the master of this spring is Mîmir, who is full of knowledge, because he drinks from it daily; once Alfödhr (Odhinn) came and asked for a sip of the spring, but he was not given permission until he had thrown one of his eyes into it as a pledge."

Thus Mîmr-Mîmir, one way or another, is Odhinn's instructor, his professor of runes; and the loss of a bodily eye was the means by which the magician-god acquired in exchange a spirit eye, the power of second sight, and all the supernatural powers that its possession brings. As Roger Caillois has pointed out, the case of Tiresias is somewhat similar, in that he too received his powers of clairvoyance at the same time he became blind. In the case of the Scandinavian god, however, even the outward mark of this profitable exchange benefits him. It is the *proof* of his powers, so that when the unknown one-eyed figure appears in battles, for example, then the moment of destiny is at hand, and those involved are left in no doubt of the fact. Thus, for Odhinn, mutilation and function are indeed interdependent: the mutilation was a payment, the resulting disfigurement an enabling certificate, empowering the god to perform his magician's function.

Tyr's Hand

The case of Tyr is comparable in part. A tale in Snorri, with which the philologists have wreaked no small havoc, but which I (along with Jan de Vries, it would appear) persist in regarding as based on early material, recounts at length how Tyr came to lose his hand (*Gylfaginning*, 35; cf. *Lokasenna*, stanzas 38 and 39). This tale tells of the binding, before he grows to full size, of the wolf Fenrir, who, according to prophecy, is fated to become the scourge of the gods.

The young wolf has already broken out of two strong chains without the slightest difficulty. Odhinn, becoming apprehensive, then turns to the Black Elves, who are ironworkers, and has them make a magic leash that looks no stronger than a silken thread. The gods invite the wolf, as though in play, to let itself be fastened and then to break the thread. The wolf suspects that this apparently harmless device has been fabricated with guile and trickery (*gört medh list ok vêl*), but the gods pursue their aim with flattery, then temptation: "If you do not succeed in breaking the leash, that will be proof that the gods have nothing to fear from you, and we will release you." The wolf still hesitates: "If you succeed in binding me so fast that I cannot free myself, then you will laugh in my face!" In the end, in order not to lose face, he accepts, but on one condition: "Let one of you place his hand in my mouth as a pledge that there will be no trickery!" (*thâ leggi einn hverr ydharr hönd sîna î munn mêr at vedhi, at thetta sê falslaust gört*). "Not one of the gods wished to pledge his hand, until Tyr held out his right [hand] and placed it in the wolf's mouth" (*ok vildi engi sîna hönd framselja, fyrr enn Tyr lêt framm haegri hönd sîna ok leggr î munn ûlfinum*). Of course, the wolf is unable to free itself. The harder it tries, the stronger the magic leash becomes. "The Ases laughed then, all save Tyr, who left his hand behind there" (*thâ hlôgu allir nema Tyr, hann lêt hönd sîna*). Thanks to this combination of the magic bond invented by Odhinn and the heroic pledge provided by Tyr, the gods are saved, and the wolf will remain leashed until the end of the world – at which time, I might add, he will wreak his revenge.

It is a serious mark of the legend's authenticity, it is scarcely necessary for me to stress, that Tyr's action is precisely of the kind appropriate to a jurist-god. An entrapping pact must be concluded with the enemy, one that entails a pledge forfeit in advance, and Tyr, alone among all the Ases, offers that pledge. The enemy is foolish enough to accept the contractual risk of an exchange in which the mere mutilation of one god is offered as compensation for utter defeat. Tyr, the heroic legal expert, seizes his opportunity. And with his sacrifice, he not only procures the salvation of the gods but also regularizes it: he renders legal that which, without him, would have been pure fraud.

I drew attention in the previous chapter to the fact that the **Tîwaz* (or Mars-Thincsus) of the continental Germans was the god who presided over the law of war, the god of war viewed as a matter of jurisprudence. The extent of that domain needs to be measured: even in earliest times, since law was already involved, the great thing must have been to keep up appearances, to act in the best interests of one's people without putting oneself in the wrong "internationally." How far is one committed when one makes a commitment? How is one to draw the enemy into one of those treaties that is as good as an ambush? How does one respect the letter of the law and yet betray the spirit of one's oath? How can one make the adversary appear to be in the wrong when he is plainly in the right? All these questions in Rome required the skill of the *fetiales* and, among the Germans, the counsel of *Tîwaz.

The One-Eyed and the One-Handed

Thus Tyr's disfigurement, like Odhinn's, is directly related to his divine function and permanent mode of action. It is possible that, in its earliest form, the myth from which Snorri's story derives had as its object the *justification* of Tyr's already-recognized juridical nature. In that case, there would be strict symmetry between the two gods, the one being the Magician because he has dared to lose his eye, the other being the Jurist because he has dared to pledge his hand. They would have become what they are in the same way that specialists were prepared for their tasks in China – a comparison much loved by Marcel Granet – by adaptive mutilation. However, even in its attested state, the tradition already gives us enough without that hypothesis. Perhaps it was not *in order* to become the divine lawyer that Tyr lost his right hand, but, it was at the very least *because* he was the lawyer that he, alone among the gods, was the one who did in fact lose his hand.

In sum, alongside **Thunraz-Thôrr* (who wins wars without resorting to finesse, by infighting, by relying on his strength alone), the two sovereign gods represent two superior techniques. **Wôdhanaz-Odhinn* terrifies the enemy, petrifies him with the glamor of his magic, while *Tyr-*Tîwaz* circumvents and disarms him with the ruses of the law. We do not know who, on the earthly level, the "men of Tyr," the guardsmen of the Germanic armies, actually were, but we have already seen who "Odhinn's men" were: the *berserkir*, the beast-warriors, invulnerable and wild, of whom Odhinn himself is the prototype, since we read of him (*Ynglingasaga*, 6): "He could make his enemies blind and deaf, or like stones with fear, and their weapons could no more cut than sticks...." Such are the various but equally efficient – one might almost say "equally elegant" – privileges of the one-eyed god and the one-handed god.

The symbolism here is probably very ancient, since Roman epic literature has preserved an invaluable variant, linked not to two "sovereigns" (the Republican orientation of these stories would not permit that), but to two "saviors of the state." I am thinking of the two famous episodes that together constitute the greater part of the Republic's first war: that of Horatius the Cyclops and that of Mucius the Left-handed. Twin episodes, one of which irresistibly summons up the other among both the historians and the moralists of antiquity, and whose interdependence is underlined even further by the fact that Cocles and Scaevola, at the conclusion of their exploits, both receive exceptional, and to some extent similar, public recognition – a last vestige, possibly, of the "sovereign" value originally attached to their modes of action and their careers.

Cocles is the one-eyed hero, the famous Horatius, who, when Lars Porsenna is about to take the city by assault, single-handedly holds the enemy in check by his strangely wild behavior, and thus wins the first phase of the war. When the city has finally been besieged and famine threatens, Scaevola is the hero who goes to Porsenna and of his own free will burns his own right hand before him, thus persuading Porsenna to grant the Romans a friendly peace that is the equivalent of a victory. The traditions relating to Odhinn and Tyr give us the key to these two little "historical" mysteries. The selfsame concept is apparent in the guise of mythical tales among the Germans and of historical narratives in Rome: above the equipoise of fortune in an ordinary battle, we have the certain victory gained by the "demoralizing radiance" of someone with "the gift," on the one hand, and, on the other, a war terminated by the heroic use of a legal procedure. Let us examine these two stories more closely.

Cocles[1]

Little inclined as they were to the supernatural, the Romans have nevertheless made it very plain that Cocles, in this combat, was more than an ordinary man; that he mastered his enemies more by the force of his personality and good luck than by any physical means; and that his enemies were unable to get near him.

Polybius, for example (*Histories*, VI, 55), even though he is the only writer to accept that Cocles was badly wounded and died after the battle, is clear on this point, despite his generally rather slapdash wording: "covered with wounds, he [Cocles] stayed at his post and checked the assault, the enemies being less struck (stupefied, *κατα-πεπληγμένων*) by his strength than by his courage and his daring."

Livy's account (II, 10) is more circumstantial and gives us a very clear picture of a situation unique in "Roman history." He depicts Cocles, amid the general debacle, rushing to the head of the bridge that is the sole access to Rome, which the Romans, taking advantage of this respite, then begin to demolish. "He stupefied the enemy by this miracle of daring" (*ipso miraculo audaciae obstupefecit hostes*). Then, remaining alone at the entrance to the bridge, he casts terrible and menacing looks at the Etruscan leaders (*circumferens truces minaciter oculos*), challenging them individually, insulting them collectively. For a long while no one dares to attack him. Then they shower him with javelins (*undique in unum hostem tela coniiciunt*); but all stick bristling in his shield, and he, stubborn and unmoved, continues with giant strides to hold the bridge (*neque ille minus obstinatus ingenti pontem obtineret gradu*...). Eventually, they decide to hurl themselves upon him, but just then the thunder of the collapsing bridge and the joyful shouts of the Romans fill them with a sudden fear and stop them in their tracks (*fragor... clamor... pavore subito impetum sustinuit*). Mission accomplished, Cocles commends himself to the god of Tiber, hurls himself fully armed into the river, and swims across it under a hail of ineffective missiles, all of which fail to hit him (*multisque superincedentibus telis incolumis ad suos tranavit*). Thus, in Livy, Cocles controls events throughout, with his terrible grimaces, which paralyze the enemy, and with his good luck, which wards off all weapons.

Dionysius of Halicarnassus (V, 24), who is more verbose and concerned with verisimilitude, at least adds the detail that Cocles was a *iunior.* He also retains this feature: "The Etruscans who pursued the Romans did not dare engage him in hand-to-hand combat (while he was occupying the bridge), regarding him as a madman and as a man in the throes of death" (*ώς μεμηνότι καί θανατῶντι*). There then follows a lengthy description of the fight, conducted at a distance, during which the unapproachable Roman victoriously returns all the projectiles with which the enemy vainly attempts to overwhelm him.

This unanimity among our authors makes it plain enough that there was something superhuman about Cocles in this battle. Properly speaking, his "gifts" are not, even in Livy, magical "eye-power" and invulnerability; but they are almost that, and they would have been precisely that if the source were not a narrative with historical pretensions, and if we were not in Rome.

It must be remarked upon that this terrible hero who blasts the Etruscans with his gaze, thereby reversing the normal course of battle, is called "Cocles," which is to say (if we follow the usual Roman interpretation), the one-eyed. It is no less remarkable that the mutilation is constantly presented as prior to the exploit. He had lost an eye, all the authors simply tell us, during a previous war. Plutarch alone (*Publicola*, 16), after having quoted this opinion first, adds an extremely interesting variant: "other writers say he owed this appellation [a distortion of the Greek "Cyclops"] to the fact that the upper part of his nose was so flattened, so deeply recessed, that there was no separation between his eyes, and his eyebrows met" (*διὰ σιμότητα τῆς ῥινὸς ἐνδεδυκυίας, ὥστε μηδὲν εἶναι τὸ διόριζον τὰ ὄμματα καὶ τὰς ὀφρῦς συγκεχύσθαι*).

In my *Mythes et dieux des Germains* (p. 105 and n.2), I drew attention to the fact that the great warriors of northern Europe – the Irish Cuchulainn, the Viking chiefs – practiced a heroic grimace that was the certificate of their power, as it were, and the proof of their victory. In Cuchulainn's case, this grimace is only one of the "signs," one of the monstrous "shapes" or "forms" (*delba*) that came upon him immediately after his initiation combat and that were manifest thereafter whenever he was gripped by warlike fury. It took the following form: "he closed one of his eyes," one text says, "until it was no bigger than the eye of a needle, while opening the other until it was as big as the rim of a mead cup" (*iadais indara suil connarbo lethiu indas cro snathaiti, asoilgg alaile combo moir beolu midchuaich*); or, according to a variant, he "swallowed one of his eyes into his head, until even a wild heron could scarcely have brought it back from the depths of his skull to the surface of his cheek," while "the other leapt out and placed itself on his cheek, on the outside" (*imsloic in dara suil do ina chend, issed mod danastarsed fiadchorr tagraim do lar a gruade a hiarthor achlocaind, sesceing a seitig co m-boi for a gruad sechtair*: for these texts and other variants see M.-L. Sjoestedt-Jonval, *Etudes Celtiques,* I, 1936, pp. 9, 10, 12, 18; also, analogous data concerning Gallic coins that I interpret differently from the author; cf. E. Windisch, *Tain Bo Cualnge*, 1905, p. 370, n.2). In the case of the Viking Egill, the grimace forms part of a heroic gesture that is, apparently, traditional, since it is understood by the person at whom it is directed. He presents himself in this grimacing shape before the king, who is bound to pay him the wages of his victories, and who, in fact, does continue to pay for as long as the Viking's countenance has not regained its natural composure: "When he sat down, he caused one of his eyebrows to leap down as far as his cheek, and the other up to his hairline; and Egill had black eyes and eyebrows that met" (*er hann sat... tha hleypdhi hann annarri bruninni ofan a kinnina, en annarri upp i harraetr; Egill var svarteygr ok skolbrunn*). It is not until he is satisfied with the payment that he abandons this "shape," and that "his eyebrows return to their places" (... *tha foru brynn hans i lag*: See *Egils Saga Skallagrimssonar,* LV, 9). These grimaces amount to a monstrous widening of one eye, while occluding the other. Both form part of a terrifying mimicry, doubtless based on a principle well known to the Harii, who, according to Tacitus (*Germania*, 43), won battles by terror alone: *terrorem inferunt, nullo hostium sustinente novum ac velut infernum adspectum; nam primi in omnibus proeliis oculi vincuntur* ("they strike terror; no enemy can face this novel and, as it were, hellish vision; in every battle, after all, the feeling of being conquered comes to the eye first"). This "ghostly army" (*feralis exercitus*) of the Harii leads us back to the Einherjar (**Aiṇa-hariya-*) and the *berserkir*, presided over by their prototype, Odhinn (cf. *Mythes et dieux des Germains*, p. 80ff.). It also seems to me probable, albeit unprovable, that Odhinn's ocular disfigurement, of which we have already seen the "civil" magic value, as it were, must also, in "military" actions, have contributed to the paralyzing terror that the *Ynglingasaga* (section 6) attributes to him as his principal weapon. In times of peace, his single eye was the pledge and the proof of his clairvoyance; in times of war, the god undoubtedly cast "the evil eye" upon those whose fate he had quite literally decreed. Ultimately, there seems little doubt that this, too, was one of the objectives shared by the ocular contortions of Egill and Cuchulainn. The congenital, or acquired, malformation attributed by Roman epic literature to its terrorizing champion, Cocles, doubtlessly is maintaining the memory of analogous and very ancient beliefs or practices in the Latin world.

Scaevola

Scaevola's links with Fides and Dius Fidius have long been recognized. I cannot do better than to reproduce the reflections of W.-F. Otto (Pauly-Wissowa, *Encyclopédie*, VI, 1909, col. 2283, under *Fides*): "Several scholars have noted that the story of Mucius Scaevola must have been connected, in some way, with the worship of Fides, and particularly with the custom, specific to that cult, of swathing the right hand. Ettore Pais has drawn attention to the fact that the temple of Dius Fidius, who is certainly akin to Fides, was located on the *collis Mucialis*, the name of which calls to mind the *gens Mucia*, and he has concluded that the myth of the burnt right hand originated in some variety of ordeal. According to Salomon Reinach (*Le voile de l'Oblation, Cultes, Mythes et Religions*, I, 1905, p. 308;

though the work originally dates from 1897), the swathing of the right hand in the cult of Fides is a symbolic offering of that hand to the goddess, and the story of Scaevola would thus refer to a time and a case in which such offerings were still made. This second interpretation seems to me inadmissible; but I cannot resign myself to separating the story of Mucius burning his right hand from the custom of swathing the right hand in the cult of Fides. Although unable to explain the legend, I should like to point out that the tradition concerning Claelia and other hostages, a tradition closely linked with that of Mucius Scaevola, is recounted as outstanding evidence of the *Fides publica populi Romani....*"

Basing himself on W.-F. Otto, M.F. Münzer (*op. cit.*, XVI, 1933, col. 417, under *Mucius Scaevola*) has made the following accurate observations: "Dionysius of Halicarnassus himself, even though his rationalism and incomprehension caused him to suppress Scaevola's self-mutilation, does draw attention to the fact that, when face-to-face with Porsenna, Mucius swears an oath forcing himself to tell the truth (V, 29, 2: *πίστεις δοὺς ἐπὶ θεῶν*), and that he receives a guarantee from Porsenna, also under oath (29, 3: *δίδωσιν αὐτῷ δὶ ὅρκων τὸ πιστόν*). Dionysius also adds that Mucius tricks Porsenna, and that his oath is a ruse, a matter that the other authors leave in the air, failing to make clear whether the revelations that Mucius makes (about the plan drawn up by three hundred young Romans to relay one another, in successive attempts to stab the enemy king – he, Mucius, being only the first to make the attempt, and to fail) are true or false. Here, perhaps, lies the original reason for the loss of Mucius's right hand: out of patriotism, and with full awareness of his action, he swore a false oath and voluntarily received the punishment for his false swearing. Thus, what could have once been celebrated as an act of heroic abnegation later came to lose any clear motivation, or ceased to have any motivation at all, when it began to seem impossible to accept the treachery and the false oath."

It is certain that Münzer is correct here, and that the central thrust of the story was originally as he describes it. But perhaps the "prototype" tradition, on which the historians of Rome were at work, with their varying sets of moral susceptibilities, was even simpler still. Let us remember the mutilation of Tyr: that mythological fiction is easily superimposed on the fragment of epic history we are considering here. For Mucius, as for Tyr, the object is to inspire trust in a threatening enemy, to make him believe something false – in both cases by sacrifice of a right hand – which will persuade that enemy to adopt a stance favorable to their own side. In risking – and thereby inevitably sacrificing – his hand, Tyr gives the gods' enemy the wolf reason to believe that the leash they wish to put on him is not a magic bond (which is false) and thus to agree to the trial. Once bound, the wolf will not be able to free itself, Tyr will lose his hand, but the gods will be saved. By voluntarily burning his hand before Porsenna, Mucius is giving Rome's enemy, the Etruscan king, reason to think that he is being truthful (even if he is lying) when he tells him that three hundred young Romans, all as resolute as himself, could very well have sacrificed their lives in advance and that, in consequence, he, Porsenna, stands every chance of perishing by one of their daggers. The fear, and also the esteem, the king suddenly feels for such a people leads him to conclude the peace treaty that saves Rome. It is true that the "pledge" mechanism is not the same in both cases; the hand that Tyr previously risks is a genuine *bailbond* for his honesty, whereas the hand that Mucius destroys then and there is a *sample* of Roman heroism. But the result is the same: both hands provide the *guarantee* of an affirmation that, without the hand, would not be believed, and that, by means of the hand, is in fact believed and thus achieves its effect on the enemy's mind.

I hasten to acknowledge that Mucius Scaevola's act, whether sullied by trickery or not, is the nobler of the two (or at least produces nobler effects): Porsenna is not deprived of the capacity, merely of the intention, to do harm. As befits a representative of the series "Mitra-Fides, etc.," Mucius is a true peacemaker who diverts the enemy's mind onto the path of an honorable truce, a durable friendship, so that the treaty concluded between the young Republic and the Etruscan king is certainly not fraudulent, and was even to be famously respected (cf. the story of Claelia), and to serve, as Mommsen and Münzer (*op. cit.*) have observed, as a model and reference point for the treaties of friendship that historical Rome was to conclude with foreign sovereigns.

This mythological consonance between Rome and the Germanic world is reinforced by a linguistic one: the Latin *vas* (genitive *vadis*), the legal term for the "pledge that stands surety for," has no corresponding word except in Germanic and Baltic, and there the corresponding word is precisely the one to be found in the Snorri text, quoted earlier: Tyr's hand is placed in the wolf's mouth *at vedhi*, "as surety," so that he will permit himself to be bound. This word (*vedh*, neuter) is the same one that still subsists in the modern German *Wette*, "wager," in the Swedish *staa vad*, "to wager," and even in the French *gage, gager*, "pledge, to wager" – a curious contamination of the Latin and Germanic forms. (On *wadium*, *Wette*, etc., on "the amphibology of the wager and the contract," and on the relation between *wadium* and *nexum*, cf. Mauss, *The Gift*, p. 60ff.).

Roman Mythology[2]

These two stories – which I have not coupled arbitrarily, since they were always consciously regarded by the Romans themselves as inseparable – are clearly seen to illuminate the Nordic facts. And this fact, in its turn, is justification for the procedure I have adopted of constantly searching in the earliest "Roman history" for the equivalent of what, under other skies, presents itself as "divine myths." It is not my concern here to take sides as to the fundamental veracity of this history. It is of little consequence to me whether, for example, kings named Romulus and Numa actually did exist, whether Romulus was assassinated, whether the Tarquinii were later "driven out," whether Lars Porsenna did besiege Rome, whether the plebeians did secede to the Sacred Hill, and so on. I am not interested in arguing about the reality of Brutus the Consul, or Publicola, or the importance that the gens Horatia and the gens Mucia might or might not have had in distant times. For me, the important thing is that the Romans should have linked certain edifying or symbolic scenes to their epic narratives of these events, and to the biographies of these characters, whatever their degree of historicity; and that the purpose of those scenes is the justification either of periodic feast days or rites (such as the Lupercalia, the *poplifugium*, the *regifugium*, the festival of Anna Perenna, etc.), or of moral behaviors or "systems of representations" still familiar in the classical era, all of which are naturally very much earlier than the real or fictitious events seen as "establishing themselves" in "history," since they are as old as, and older than, Roman society itself. We must accustom ourselves to the notion that, given such wan gods who are almost wholly lacking in adventures – as Dionysius of Halicarnassus observed in his *Roman Antiquities* (II, 18) – the true Roman mythology, the mythology articulated in narratives, in circumstantiated events, is a mythology of heroes, epic in form, and little different – its weighty concern for verisimilitude apart – from the Irish mythology of the Middle Ages. Let none of my critics attempt to saddle me with the ridiculous thesis that the "Roman-Etruscan" or "Publicola-Porsenna" conflicts were the "historicization" of an ancient mythology of the Indian or Greek type, in which gods struggle against demons. No, Scaevola's opponent has not "taken the place" of a demon! What I do think is that, from its very beginnings, from the time when it acquired those specific characteristics that led to its success, Rome conceived its myths on the terrestrial plane, as a dynamic balance between terrestrial actors and forces.

Nuada and Lug

A moment ago I mentioned Irish mythology; and it is by no means out of place in this investigation, since it too presents us with a version of the "one-eyed sovereign" and the "one-armed sovereign" antithesis. In the epic representation of the successive invasions and settlements of Ireland, the Tuatha De Danann, which is to say, the ancient gods, on whom the Irish concentrated what they had retained of the Indo-European myths, conquered the island from the demonic Formorians and their allies the Fir Bolg, the Fir Domnann and the Galioin. Their two leaders in this conquest were Nuada (or Nuadu) and Lug, two ancient and well-known gods. One had been the *Nodens, Nodons*, whose name occurs in Latin inscriptions in Great Britain; the other is the great *Lug samildanach* ("sym-poly-technician"), who gave his name to Lugnasad, the Irish seasonal festival, and to the Gallic city of Lugdunum.

Tradition describes the installation of the Tuatha De Danann in Ireland as occurring in two phases. There were two successive battles, two victories, achieved a few years apart in the same place, on the plain called Mag Tured; the first over the Fir Bolg, the Fir Domnann and the Galioin, and the second over the Fomorians. Philologists, however, are generally of the opinion that this chronology is the result of a late and artificial doubling, and that there was originally only a single battle, that which became "the second." On the face of it, their argument is that the two earliest catalogues of Ireland's epic literature, as well as the "Glossary of Cormac" (about 900 A.D.), mention only "a" battle of Mag Tured, and that it is not until texts of the eleventh century that two battles are mentioned and expressly differentiated (d'Arbois de Jubainville, *The Irish Mythological Cycle*, Dublin, 1903 pp. 84-86; cf., with slight attenuation, *L'Epopée celtique en Irlande*, 1892, p. 396). But the real and underlying reason is that this duality of battles seems, to them, both nugatory and meaningless, and that, in addition, the epic material of the first battle is as jejune and insignificant as that of the second is fertile and original.

The philological argument is a weak one. First, it might well be that the first battle was in fact known at an early date, *without giving rise to autonomous epic narratives* such as those recorded in the early catalogues, and that it was referred to in narratives dealing with the second battle solely in order to clarify a detail or a situation. Second, the *fragment* inserted in the "Glossary of Cormac" does certainly refer to the "second" battle, waged against the Fomorians (d'Arbois de Jubainville, p. 85 n. 3); but how does that prove that the existence of the first battle was unknown in about 900 A.D.? Was Cormac obliged to mention everything? Similarly, the Cinaed poem contains a brief allusion to a well-known preliminary of the second battle and situates it, without further clarification, "before the battle of Mag Tured" (*ria cath Maigi Tuired*); but why *should* he specify "before the *second* battle"? Third, a poet contemporary with Cinaed, Eochaid ua Flainn (died, 984), was already aware of the first battle, since he says of that battle, in which a hundred thousand warriors were slain, that it ended the royal line of the Tuath Bolg (i.e., clearly, the Fir Bolg). And this presupposes that the division explicitly indicated in the later tradition was already acquired (first battle: Tuatha De Danann versus Fir Bolg; second battle: Tuatha De Danann versus Fomorians).

As for the philologists' underlying reason for eliminating the first battle, the considerations of this present chapter annul it, or rather provide a very serious argument against it. If there are two successive victories at Mag Tured, it is because, as in the war against Porsenna and the exploits of Cocles and Scaevola, there are two types of victorious warrior to be given individual prominence: in the first, Nuada leads his people to victory, but *loses his right arm in so doing* – and this accident is immediately made use of in *a ruse based on the law of war*, which in turn leads to *a compromise peace and a pact of amity* between the adversaries. In the second battle, Lug ensures success for the selfsame people *with magic*, by circling around his army *while taking on the appearance of a one-eyed man*, and this time *the victory is total, without compromise.*

The second of these episodes is well known (*Second Battle of Mag Tured*, ed. W. Stokes, *Revue Celtique*, XII, 1891 p. 96ff.). The Tuatha De Danann are already partially established in Ireland as a result of the first battle, but, feeling themselves oppressed by Bress and the Fomorians, they have shaken off their yoke. The great battle is about to begin. The Tuatha De Danann, who have designated Lug as their commander-in-chief (section 83), are unwilling to place in peril a life and a fund of knowledge so invaluable to them (section 95). Then (section 129), "the Tuatha De Danann, on the other side, rose up, left nine of their comrades to guard Lug, and went to do battle. Then, when the combat had begun, Lug, together with his driver, escaped from the guard under which he had been placed, so that he appeared at the head of the Tuatha De Danann army. A hard and fierce battle was fought between the Fomorians and the men of Ireland. Lug strengthened the men of Ireland (*boi Lug og nertad fer n-Erenn*), exhorting them to fight bravely so that they might live in servitude no longer; it was better for them to meet death defending their country than to live in subjugation and pay tribute, as they had been doing. That is why Lug then sang this song, while he circled the men of Ireland on one foot and with one eye (*conid and rocan Lug an cetul so sios for lethcois ocus letsuil timchall fer n-Erenn*; cf. above Cuchulainn's one-eyed *delb*):

A battle shall arise....

(Section 130): "The armies let out a great shout as they went into combat, and so on." And then comes victory (sections 131-138), dearly bought but crushing and final, for the army of Lug, who is made king, Nuada having been killed at the very outset.

The first episode is less famous, doubtless because of the prejudice against it noted earlier. Here it is, as recounted in the unique and late manuscript published by M.J. Fraser (*Eriu*, VIII, 1916, pp. 4-59), which, despite its verbose form conforming to the taste of decadent epic literature, might of course retain early material. The Tuatha De Danann have just landed in Ireland. They have requested that the natives, the Fir Bolg, cede one half of the island. The Fir Bolg have refused, and a fierce battle ensues. In the course of battle (section 48), the Fir Bolg named Sreng "struck the 'paramount king,' Nuada, with his sword; he cut through the edge of his buckler and the right arm at the shoulder, so that the arm fell to the earth with a third of the buckler (*dobert Sreang bem cloidimh don airdrigh .i. do Nuadhaid gur theasg bile an sgeth ogus an laimh ndes ac a ghualaind, gu ndrochair an lamh gu triun an sgeth le for talmain*). The Tuatha De Danann carry Nuada from the battlefield and fight on so valiantly that they end that day victorious. So victorious, apparently, that should the struggle be resumed the next day, the Fir Bolg face certain extermination. During the night, despondent and downcast, the Fir Bolg hold council. Should they leave Ireland? Accept partition? Or fight on (section 57)? They agree on the third option. But Sreng appears to deplore this bloody and futile resistance: "Resistance, for men, is destruction," he says in verse, "the plains of Ireland are filled with suffering; for its forests we have met with misfortune, the loss of many brave men." As a result (section 58), when the two armies are drawn up, Sreng challenges his victim of the previous day, Nuada, to single combat. "Nuada looked at him bravely, as if he were sound in body (*atracht Nuada co nertchalma, amail dobeth slan*), and said to him: 'If what you seek is a fair fight (*comlann comadais*), strap down your right arm, for I no longer have mine (*cengailter luth de laime desi, uair nach fuil sin oramsa*); in this way, the fight will be fair!' Sreng replied: 'Your state implies no obligation on my side (*ni tormaig sin fiacha etir oramsa*), for our first fight has been canceled out (*uair robo comthrom ar cetchomrag*), that is the rule agreed between us!'" This threat to Nuada, this blackmail, as it were, leads the Tuatha De Danann to take the initiative in reaching a compromise that will limit their success. After meeting in council, they offer Sreng the choice of any province in Ireland for himself and his people. Thus peace is concluded, "peace and agreement and friendship" (*sith ogus comand ogus cairdine*). Sreng and the Fir Bolg choose the province of Connaught, the province of the paramount king, which consoles them for their real defeat with the appearance of "success" (*co haindinid aithesach*). As we have seen, Nuada survives, but is forced to give up his kingship to a temporary king (Bress), while he has an artificial arm made in order to reclaim his kingship. Hence, his appellation "Nuada Airgetlam," or "Nuada of the Silver Hand."

If we now go back to the diptych of legends that makes up the war of the Romans against Porsenna, the differences between it and the paired Celtic narratives are easily perceived. First, the order of the episodes is reversed: Cocles and his wild looks preceded Scaevola and his burned hand, whereas Nuada and his severed arm precede Lug and his magic grimace. Second, the episodes of Cocles and Scaevola are two episodes in a single war, which, thanks to Scaevola, is definitively ended by the pact of peace and friendship, whereas the Tuatha De Danann fight two successive wars, the first ended by a peace pact, the second by the extermination of their enemy. Third, Scaevola's mutilation is voluntary, calculated; it is Scaevola himself who makes juridical use of it, persuading Porsenna to come to terms, despite his imminent victory: whereas Nuada loses his arm by accident, and the exploitation of that accident is initiated by the Fir Bolg, who are facing disaster, rather than by the Tuatha De Danann, who, while facing a threat to their king's life, are nevertheless in practice already victorious.[3]

All this is true; but the analogies are no less perceptible. First, the chronological reversal of the episodes in no way alters their meaning. Second, although the Irish epic speaks of two wars, those wars are waged with only a short interval between them, and are merely two complementary, interdependent episodes in the Tuatha De Danann's settlement of Ireland. Moreover, the second war is declared in the name of liberty (cf. Lug's exhortations to his troops quoted earlier), as the Tuatha De Danann have thrown off the yoke of a semi-alien and wholly tyrannical king, Bress, whom the Fomorians wish to replace – which is precisely the situation of the Romans in relation to Porsenna, who wants to reinstate Tarquinius Superbus (cf. the insults hurled by Cocles at the Etruscans in Livy, II, 10). Third, however dissimilar the "exploitations" of Scaevola's burnt hand and Nuada's severed arm might be, the fact remains that this exploitation takes place, that it culminates in a compromise peace and friendship (as in the case of Porsenna) which is, above all, juridical: using legalistic arguments, and rejecting the case against it formulated by Nuada, Sreng demands his *right in law*, which is to resume the duel begun the day before, with its "score" exactly as it was at the end of the first "set," which he had won, as it were, "hands down." And it is under pressure from this harsh but legitimate requirement that the Tuatha De Danann, after deliberation, make peace with the Fir Bolg.

Therefore, it seems to me that the two battles of Mag Tured are early; that, from the viewpoint of a philosophy of sovereignty inherited by the Celts, as by the Latins, from their Indo-European ancestors, they are necessary; and that they preserve, in an original fictional form, the double symbolism of the one-eyed sovereign and the one-handed sovereign. Additionally, such a stance also avoids the serious difficulties that arise if one accepts the argument that there originally was only a *single* battle of Mag Tured. I will give one example. Unless we suppose (and where would that lead us?) that the story of the single original battle had a quite different structure from the narrative that has come down to us of the second battle, how are we to situate within that single battle the *mutilation* of Nuada, since he also, we are told, *perishes* in it and must of necessity perish in it? His appellation "of the Silver Hand" clearly requires an interval between the loss of his hand and his death. Yet how can we accept that Nuada survived a battle constructed wholly in honor of Lug, which had as its consequence, both logical in itself and asserted by tradition, that Lug became the new king of the Tuatha De Danann and, therefore, Nuada's successor?

It is from this new point of view we ought to resume the old argument, always conducted on shaky grounds, for and against the linking of "Nuada of the Silver Hand" with the one-handed Tyr (In favor: Axel Olrik, *Aarb. f. oldk.*, 1902, p. 210ff.; J. de Vries *Altgerm. Religionsgesch.*, II, 1937, p. 287. Against, with very weak arguments or most improbable hypotheses: K. Krohn, *Tyrs högra hand, Freys svärd*, in *Festsk. H.F. Feilberg*, 1911, p. 541ff.; Al. H. Krappe, *Nuada à la main d'argent*, in *Rev. Celt.*, XLIX, 1932, p. 91ff.); the link holds good.

We know that a late Mabinogi conserves, in the form "Lludd of the Silver Hand," *Lludd Llaw Ereint* (a description without explanation today),[4] the Welsh equivalent of *Nuada Airgetlam*. It is worthy of note that this Mabinogi, *The Adventure of Llud and Llevelys*, (Loth, *Les Mabinogion*, ed. of 1913, I, pp. 231-241) presents Lludd not just on his own, but as a couple, two brother-kings, Lludd (king of Britain) and Llevelys (king of France). King Lludd is a great builder (of London), a fine warrior, a generous distributor of food, but he is unable to solve the problem of three mysterious scourges that invade and lay waste his island. He consults Llevelys, "known for the excellence of his councils and his wisdom," and it is Llevelys who explains to him the magic origin of the three scourges, as well as providing him with the magic means to be rid of them. Ought we to see, concealed by a final distortion behind Llevelys, an equivalent of the Irish Lug (who is certainly to be found in the *Mabinogi of Math*, under the name of *Lleu*)?

Chapter X

Savitṛ and Bhaga

Sovereignty: the General Staff

The topic we are exploring does not permit the mind to rest for long upon the states of balance it has glimpsed. Not that the new elements introduced into one's research at each new stage destroy the results of the preceding stage. The contrary is true. But those results can then no longer be viewed as anything but particular cases or as fragments of a much larger ensemble. Thus my analysis of the Luperci, then that of the flamines, at first pursued in isolation, eventually revealed a new perspective: that of the opposition and the "complementarity" of the two types of sacred persons (chapters 1 and 2). This antithetical couple, in its turn, took its place within an abundant collection of other linked couples – conceptual, ritual or mythical – that together define a bipartite representation of sovereignty (chapters 2 and 3). The implications of this then led me to look more closely at the Indo-European hierarchy of social functions, and I observed that this "bipartition" was not a specific characteristic of the first function, but that, by a sort of dialectical deduction, the entire social and cosmic hierarchy was made up of similar opposing pairs, successively harmonized into wider and wider concepts (chapter 4). This view might well have appeared to be definitive, since I only went on to examine the interaction and activities of the sovereign couple within the various settings of sovereignty – in a kind of philosophy of royal histories (chapter 5), in civil law (chapter 6), in the economic administration of the world (chapter 8), in war (chapter 9); and also, as a parallel, in the Indo-European areas of the world outside of Rome, India and Iran: among the Greeks (chapter 7), the Germanic peoples (chapters 7, 8, and 9) and the Celts (chapter 9). At this point, however, a detail from these latest inquiries abruptly forces me to widen the focus yet again.

Mitra and Varuṇa indisputably form a couple. But that couple is not isolated at the head of the divine hierarchy: around it, at the same level, its equal (in dignity if not in vigor), Vedic India, sets a group of singular beings called the Āditya, so that Mitra and Varuṇa are in fact no more than the two most typical, and most frequently invoked, of the Āditya as a whole. Just as my work on Uranos-Varuṇa left in shadow an essential aspect of sovereignty – the aspect of the *couple* – so I can foresee that the present work has left in shadow a whole sheaf of problems: those that pertain to the relations of the couple with the other Āditya, either individually or, it might be, in groups. At the moment, I lack the means to embark upon this immense field of study with any hope of useful results. It must suffice if I draw attention to the fact that several of the Āditya bear names that are certainly very ancient. Aryaman is Indo-Iranian and might have figures corresponding to him in India (the hero *Eremon*) and in the Germanic world. Bhaga is Indo-Iranian and homophonous with *Bogu*, the noun for "god" in general throughout the Slavonic languages. Further, several of these personages bear abstract names that define their functions, and it is clear that those functions are in fact functions of sovereignty: *Bhaga* and *Aṃśa* are both linked to "distribution"; *Dhātṛ* is a "teacher," *Dakṣa*, "intelligence"; *Aryaman* himself certainly presided over important forms of social or human relations, possibly those linked with "nationality" (V. Paul

Thieme, *der Fremdling im Ṛgveda, eine Studie über die Bedeutung der Worte* ari, arya, Aryaman *und* ārya, Leipzig, 1938).

The Aməš Spənta, the personified abstractions surrounding the supreme Iranian god, are not homologous with the Āditya. Rather, they are a sublimation of the early hierarchy of Indo-Iranian functional gods, Mitra-Varuṇa, Indra and the twin Nāsatya.[1] Nevertheless, if we consider, after the Gāthās, the Avesta and Pahlavi literature as a whole, they do form a sort of general staff or board of management of sovereignty above the band of the Yazata, and embody, for example, the single high god's various modes of action throughout the tripartite universe and society.

If my analyses of Rome's "historical mythology" are correct, a comparable situation might be discerned there: Romulus and Numa, the two sovereign founders of the city, the worshippers of Jupiter and Fides, are neither its only kings nor even the only two founders of its state institutions. Each of their successors symbolizes, as do Romulus and Numa, a "type" of kingship, perfects some social organ, and is sometimes defined by a predilection for a particular cult. I am thinking in particular here, of Servius Tullius, organizer of the *census* and worshipper of Fortuna, to whom, it is quite true, he owed everything.[2] But I am also mindful of the warlike Tullus Hostilius, the "manager" of certain forms of combat (Horatius and the Curiatii),[3] and of the pious Ancus Marcius, who, at least in Livy, is not merely a repeat version of his grandfather, Numa, since the institution of the legal forms of war, of sacred diplomacy, is allotted to him.[4] Roman "history" thus distributed among successive reigns either the secondary provinces of sovereignty – those that do not coincide with the two antithetical provinces already expressed successively in the reigns of Romulus and Numa – or activities carried on in those areas where the two lower functions impinge upon sovereignty.

Let me hasten to make it plain, however, that things are actually even less simple than that: while certainly not "insertable" into the list of Rome's kings, Cocles and Scaevola, as we have seen, nevertheless express two aspects of sovereignty in its relation to combat, to victory. And in India we find a very important being, one who often forms a closely linked couple with the Āditya Bhaga, who is often associated with those other Āditya Varuṇa, Mitra and Aryaman, and who was, nevertheless, not counted in early times as an Āditya himself: I mean Savitṛ.

Savitṛ and Bhaga

The twin expressions *Savitā Bhagaḥ* and *Bhagaḥ Savitā* are customary usages in the hymns. It is true that one could regard one of these two names, in either of the two forms, as being a simple epithet describing the other ("the distributing impeller" or "the impelling distributor"), but, even reduced in this way, the expressions must attest at least to an affinity between the two personages. And, in fact, not only in the rhetoric of the hymns but also in their ritual use, Savitṛ and Bhaga do appear as complementary figures. The antithesis is less firm and, above all, less rich, than in the case of Varuṇa and Mitra – simply, no doubt, because Bhaga and Savitṛ are less well known to us and play smaller roles – but it is nevertheless clear and also consonant with the etymology of the names.

Savitṛ is an agent-noun in *-tṛ* formed on the root of Vedic *suváti* (Avestic *hu-nā-(i)ti*), "to excite, to set in motion, to vivify," sometimes "to procure," which is precisely the root used on numerous occasions, either alone or in compound forms, to denote the particular action of this god. J. Muir (*Original Sanskrit Texts*, V, 1870, p. 162ff.) has listed and examined all the strophes or lines of the *Ṛg Veda* in which this propulsive, motivating, animating power is expressed, in its various specific guises. I do not think that present-day Indianists can have much to add to his account. Sometimes – when it comes into the orbit of Prajāpati – this "propulsion" even goes as far as "creation" (see A.A. Macdonell, Vedic Mythology, Strassburg, Trübner, 1897, p. 33). Last, there seem to be links, symbolically at least, with night, or with dawn and dusk: Savitṛ is said to be the name of the sun before it rises (Sāyaṇa, *Commentary on the Ṛg Veda*, V, 81, 4), and it is said of him that he "sends to sleep" (*Ṛg Veda*, IV, 53, 6; VII, 45, 1).

Bhaga, on the contrary, neither animates nor creates, but is described as the "distributor" (*vidhartṛ*), or "apportioner" (*vibhaktṛ*). He does indeed "give shares" in wealth, and appears, in both rituals and magic hymns, to be linked to "distributive chance or luck," as for instance in the case of marriage ("husband-giver" in *Atharva Veda*, II, 36, etc.) or of agricultural prosperity (*Gobhila Gṛhyasūtra*, IV, 4, 28). Lastly, he has undisputed links with dawn ("his sister," *Ṛg Veda*, I, 123, 5) and with morning (Yāska, *Nirukta*, 12, 13).

Thus, in the wake of Varuṇa-Mitra, we find a "motor"-"distributor" couple of which the components are related in an analogous way, and are susceptible, moreover, of taking on the same figurative images (night-day). However, the domains covered by Savitṛ-Bhaga are, needless to say, more circumscribed (in Bhaga's case, they are almost entirely economic), and, "dynamic" though he may be, Savitṛ certainly does not figure as a "terrible" god associated with a "benevolent" one.

Now, it so happens that Bhaga is the god who has lost his eyes and Savitṛ the god who has lost his hands.

The God Without Eyes and the God Without Hands

The stories that account for these two interdependent disfigurements are not, as among the Germans or the Romans, related to war or to political life. Just as it tended to make the sovereigns Mitra and Varuṇa into master and avenger in the field of *ritual* and its correct observance, so the sacrificial literature of the brahmans took over Bhaga, Savitṛ and their misadventure: it was on the occasion of a *sacrifice* – something that Savitṛ normally "propels" and Bhaga "apportions" – on the occasion of a very ancient sacrifice, offered by the gods, that the two were mutilated; and it would seem that it was in recompense for those mutilations that they were both subsequently empowered, using "replacement organs," to carry out their functions in the sacrifices offered by mankind.

This orientation of the Indian story does not, however, destroy its analogies with Western legends concerning the one-eyed sovereign and the one-armed sovereign, any more than the fact that the Indian gods, unlike the Western gods or heroes, lose both eyes and both arms. Or, lastly, any more than the fact – quite normal in India, where there is a fondness for "series" – that a third mutilated figure (without teeth) or indeed a whole sequence of them should have been added to the first pair. There is, on the other hand, a more serious difference, one that totally reverses the import of the two mutilations: it is Savitṛ, the propellant god, who loses his hands, and it is Bhaga, the distributive god, who loses his eyes. Of course, it is easy enough to perceive the relationship of these losses with the two gods' functions (the hand drives, the eye allocates; cf. the bandage that we place over Fortune's eyes to signify that she is blind); but in the West it is the "jurist" god (and thus the one akin to, if not homologous with, Bhaga) who is one-armed, by reason of the recognized link between the right hand and good faith, and it is the magician god or the terrible hero who is one-eyed, by reason of the recognized link between the eye and second sight. Thus, the Indians oriented and allotted the elements of the double symbol in a completely different way. Now let me give an account of the various forms the incident took.

The *Kauṣītaki Brāhmaṇa*, VI, 13, links it to the precautions taken by the officiating brahman to consume the *prāśitra*, "the first fruit of the sacrifice." When the gods set out their sacrifice of old, they offered the first fruit to Savitṛ; it cut off his hands (*tasya pāṇī praciccheda*), and they gave him two golden hands, which is why he is called "of the golden hands" (*hiraṇyapāṇiḥ*), an epithet indeed applied to Savitṛ in the *Ṛg Veda*. Then they offered it to Bhaga; it destroyed his two eyes, which is why it is said "Bhaga is blind" (*andhaḥ*). Then they offered it to *Pūṣan*, and it knocked out his teeth, which is why it is said "Pūṣan has no teeth, he eats karambha" (a moist flour cake). Then they offered it to Indra, saying: "Indra is the strongest, the most victorious of the gods," and, using the magic formula (*brahmaṇā*), "he made it gentle." Forewarned by this unpleasant incident from divine prehistory, the brahman who in later times consumed the *prāśitra* took care to say: "I gaze on you with the eye of Mitra," "By permission of the lightfilled Savitṛ, I take you with the arms of the Aśvin, with the hands of Pūṣan," "I eat you with the mouth of Agni." Finally, he rinses his mouth with water, then touches all the parts and orifices of his body, thus restoring any damage done by consumption of the *prāśitra* (cf. a similar formula in which Savitṛ is invoked during the initiation ceremonies of the young *dvija*: *Pāraskara Gṛhyasūtra*, II, 4, 8).

The meaning of the story is clear, and Weber, in *Indische Studien* (II, 1883, pp. 307-308), provides a good explication. Briefly, the *prāśitra* is charged with sacred values, and, so, clearly cannot be jettisoned without catastrophe; but its consumption is likewise a matter of grave peril. This tragic dilemma, from which the gods were once rescued by the devotion of several of their number, is much the same as those from which the Ases and the Romans are rescued by the sacrifices of Tyr and Scaevola. It is simply that here the forces to be confronted and neutralized are purely ritual, reduced entirely to the "sacrificial discharge," whereas the forces threatening Rome and the Ases are those of their enemies – the military force of the Etruscans, the demonic force of Fenrir. Moreover, it is possible that India did have a variant closer to the Western legends, for Mahīdhāra, in his commentary on the *Vājasaneyi Saṃhitā* (I, 16; p. 21 in Weber's edition), in order to explain the epithet "of the golden hands" (*hiraṇyapāṇiḥ*), habitually applied to Savitṛ, says:

"It is because the ornaments on his fingers are of gold; or else because Savitṛ's hands, having been cut off by the demons when he was taking the *prāśitra*, the gods made him two more out of gold; that is why it is said that Savitṛ has golden hands (*yad vā daityaih prāśitraharena chinnau savitṛpānī devair hiranyamayau kṛtāv iti savitur hiraṇyapāṇītvam iti*).

Other texts recount the incident much as it occurs in the *Kauṣītaki Brāhmaṇa*, but sometimes with variants. Although the *Gopatha Brāhmaṇa* (II, 1, 2) reproduces the same sequence of mutilations, albeit with Bhaga preceding Savitṛ, the *Śátapatha Brāhmaṇa* (I, 7, 4, 6-8) restricts mutilation to Bhaga (*andhaḥ*, "blind" because he looked at the *prāśitra*) and Pūṣan (*adantakaḥ*, "toothless" because he tasted it), and it is Bṛhaspati, thanks to the "animator" Savitṛ, and not Indra, who succeeds in taming the perilous portion without injury. In general, the episode comes at the end of a "terrible" story (e.g., *Śatapatha Brāhmaṇa* I, 7, 4, 1-5): Prajāpati, the Lord of Creatures, the Creator, was guilty of having conceived a love for his own daughter. The angry gods asked Rudra, king of the beasts, to pierce him with an arrow. Rudra shot his arrow, and Prajāpati fell. Their anger stilled, the gods tended him and drew out Rudra's arrow, but, "Prajāpati being the sacrifice," a little sacrificial matter remained stuck to the arrow, and it was this that constituted the prototype of the fearsome *prāśitra*.

Fictionalized in a different form, this is the story, famous in the epic literature, of the "sacrifice of Dakṣa." Dakṣa – one of the ancient Āditya, whose name appears to mean "intelligence, skill," and who assimilated very early on into Prajāpati as universal father – offers a sacrifice to which, for variable reasons, he fails to invite Śiva (assimilated to Rudra, etc.). Śiva appears in a fury, bow in hand, and scatters the sacrifice and mutilates the gods who are present. The *Mahābhārata*, for example (X, 18), says that "Rudra cut off both Savitṛ's hands and, in his anger, put out both Bhaga's eyes, and smashed in Pūṣan's teeth with the curved end of his bow; then the gods and the various elements of the sacrifice fled..." (slokas 801-802). Eventually, this terrible Great God is appeased: "He gave back his two eyes to Bhaga, his two hands to Savitṛ, and his teeth to Pūṣan, and to the gods their sacrifice," of which they hurriedly hand over to him, as his share, "the totality" (slokas 807-808).

Other texts present slightly different versions, often omitting Savitṛ and his hands, while, on the contrary, decapitating Dakṣa, who then receives a ram's head as compensation. But, occasionally, one comes across a direct echo of the "warning formulas" of the *Kauṣītaki Brāhmaṇa*. In the *Bhāgavata Purāṇa* (IV, 7, 3-5), for example, when the terrible god is appeased and is making good the injuries he has inflicted, he tells Bhaga to look upon his share of the sacrifice "through the eye of Mitra" (*Mitrasya cakṣuṣā*), and, without mentioning Savitṛ's specific mutilation, the compensation he offers for it is precisely that found in the ancient ritual text: "Let those who lost arms and hands find arms again by the arms of the Aśvin, by the hands of Pūṣan!" (*bāhubhyām aśvinoḥ pūṣno hastābhyaṃ kṛtabāhavaḥ bhavantu*!).[5]

Such were the ways in which the twin mutilations of the ancient sovereign gods evolved in the epic literature and the Puranas. And note should be taken of Bhaga's compensation for his blinding: he will see "with the eye of Mitra." This link, this two-way connection between the "distributor" and the "punctilious" is not surprising, and echoes that which is sometimes observed – in a purely ritual context – between the "propeller" and the "terrible," between Savitṛ and Varuṇa (e.g., *Śatapatha Brāhmaṇa*, XII, 7, 2, 17). It also lends full significance to the fact that Mithra, in one part of Iran, seems to have been honored under the name *Baga* (whereas, elsewhere, *Baga* became, as in Slavonic, a generic term for "gods").

The Cyclopes and the Hundred-Handed Giants

Thus, with a reversal of the relations and an amplification of the details that alter neither the framework nor the general import of the episode, India, like the West, was no stranger to the theme of the coupled sovereign gods, or coupled "agents of sovereignty," one with mutilated eyes, the other with mutilated hands. Such agreement leads one to think that this theme was customary in the symbolism and mythology of cosmic sovereignty, as early as the time of the Indo-European community. And one is then tempted to attribute both importance and antiquity to a detail in the Uranides story. Let me just quote the beginning of Apollodorus's *Biblioteca*.

"Uranos was the first sovereign of the universe (*Οὐρανὸς πρῶτος τοῦ παντὸς ἐδυνάστευσε κόσμου*). He married Gaia and had as first children those called the 'hundred-hands,' Briareos, Gyes, Kottos, all without rivals in their stature and strength, furnished with a hundred arms (*χεῖρας μὲν ἀνὰ ἑκατόν*) and fifty heads. Then came the Cyclopes, Arges, Steropes, Brontes, each with one eye in his forehead (*ὧν ἕκαστος εἶχεν ἕνα ὀφθαλμὸν ἐπὶ τοῦ μετώπου*). These last Uranos chained, and hurled them into Tartarus (*τούτους μὲν Οὐρανὸς δήσας εἰς Τάρταρον ἔρριψε*), a place of darkness in Hades, as far from earth as earth is from heaven. Then he begot, with Gaia, sons who are called Titans: Oceanos, Koios, Hyperion, Krios, Iapetos and, last of all, Kronos, as well as daughters who are called Titanides, Tethys, Rhea, Themis, Mnemosyne, Phoibe, Dione, Theia.

"Outraged by the loss of her children who were cast into Tartarus, Gaia persuaded the Titans to attack their father and gave Kronos a steel scythe. Oceanos excepted, the Titans attacked their father, and Kronos cut off his genitals and hurled them into the sea. The Erinyes, Alekto, Tisiphone, and Magaera were born from the drops of blood that fell. Having toppled Uranos from power, the Titans brought their brothers back from Tartarus and gave Kronos power.

"But he chained them once more, and sent them back to Tartarus (*ὁ δὲ τούτους μὲν ἐν τῷ Ταρτάρῳ πάλιν δήσας καθεῖρξε*), then married his sister, Rhea. Kronos swallowed all those who were born to him, Hestia first, then Demeter and Hera, then Pluto and Poseidon, because Gaia and Uranos had prophesied that power would be taken from Kronos by his own son. Angered, Rhea journeyed to Crete, for she was pregnant with Zeus, and gave birth in Dikte's cave. [Then follows the usual story of Zeus's childhood, the stone given to the father and swallowed as a substitute, etc.]

"When Zeus was grown, he secured the aid of Metis, daughter of Oceanos, who caused Kronos to drink a drug that made him vomit up the stone, and then all the children he had swallowed. Then Zeus waged war against Kronos and the Titans. They fought for ten years. Gaia prophesied victory for Zeus if he won the allegiance of those who had been cast into Tartarus (*ἡ Γῆ τῷ Διὶ ἔχρησε τὴν νίκην, τούς καταταρταρωθέντας ἂν ἔχῃ συμμάχους*). Zeus killed Kampe, who tended their shackles, and unbound them (*ὁ δὲ τὴν φρουροῦσαν αὐτῶν τὰ δεσμὰ Κάμπην ἀποκτείνας ἔλυσε*). Then the Cyclopes gave thunder and lightning to Zeus, the skin helmet to Pluto, the trident to Poseidon. Thus armed, these three overcame the Titans, and, having imprisoned them in Tartarus, set the hundred-hands over them as their keepers (*καθείρξαντες αὐτοὺς ἐν τῷ Ταρτάρῳ τοὺς Ἑκατόγχειρας κατέστησαν φύλακας*). They, themselves, drew lots for power: Zeus received sovereignty over the sky, Poseidon over the sea, and Pluto over Hades."

I am happy to reproduce this text here for several reasons. First, in the light of all the documentary evidence so far assembled relating to the *bond*, to the importance of the bond as a symbol and as a weapon of the terrible sovereign, as opposed to both the warrior-god and the jurist-sovereign (for Varuṇa, see my *Ouranos-Varuṇa*, pp. 50-51, and *Flamen-Brahman*, pp. 67-68; for *Wôdhanaz, see my *Mythes et dieux des Germains*, pp. 21, 26-27, and above; for Romulus, see above). I hope that certain Hellenists will not continue to regard the verb *δεῖν*, the substantive *δεσμός*, and the verb *λύειν*, which occur so regularly in this narrative, as mere "every day" words. The literary trustee of a tradition whose former breadth and scope I have never claimed he was aware of, Apollodorus makes the contrast as clear as possible between two modes of struggle: that of the terrible sovereigns, Zeus's predecessors, and that of Zeus himself. Uranos – and this is partly true of his doublet, Kronos, too – does not fight and has no weapon. No mention is made of any resistance to his violence, and, yet, at least some of his victims are said to be "without rivals for their stature and their strength." This is as if to say that resistance to Uranos is inconceivable, as is attested again by the very scenario of his fall: he cannot be attacked, nor even accosted, except through the use of guile and ambush. When he takes the initiative, "he binds," and that is that. Zeus, on the contrary, is a combatant, one who fights for ten years and more against savage resistance, one who acquires weapons, and who, in order to recruit allies, "unbinds" those "bound" by Uranos, after first killing the tender of their "bonds." This opposition is in perfect conformity with that observed in India, between the magician-sovereign Varuṇa, who binds without combat, and the combatant Indra, who is only too ready to unbind Varuṇa's victims; with that observed in Germany, between binding magician, *Wôdhanaz, and the combatant, Thor; and with that observed in Rome, between the binder Romulus (who has his *lictores* bind instantly all those he points out) and either the unbinding flamen dialis or the consul of the legend of the *nexi soluti.* It is the symbolic expression of an opposition between the natures of two types of leader. And since the very names of Uranos and Varuṇa seem to be linked, according to Indian tradition, to a root that means "to bind," it is not possible for me, either by way of comparative research or simple textual analysis, to allow this extremely articulate document to be ruled out on the pretext of a mere subjective impression of "everydayness."[6]

However, I have quoted the Uranides story for another reason. I have been led to the conclusion that the Indo-Europeans symbolized two aspects of sovereignty in beings – major or minor sovereign gods, or auxiliaries to the sovereign gods – one of whom had only one eye (or no eyes at all), and the other only one hand (or no hand at all); and this deformity, usually acquired but sometimes congenital, is precisely what fits them both for their sovereign function (see the dission on Cocles, according to Plutarch's alternative explanation, above).

Now, the story of the Uranides – and not in Apollodorus alone – brings into play, first as children and as victims of the terrible Uranos, then as "givers of sovereignty" allied with Zeus, *two symmetrical groups of beings, one of which has only one eye and the other a hundred hands.* Yes, I know that there is a difference between a hundred and one. Nonetheless, it is striking that Zeus's sovereignty should be assured by the cooperation of coupled sets of abnormal beings whose abnormalities relate to the eyes, in one case, and to the hands, in the other. Perhaps there even remains, between these two groups, something of an early allocation of "secondary sovereign functions" comparable to that seen elsewhere, with those functions simply downgraded, becoming mere craft-level magic for one set, and police or prison-officer work for the other. For it is the metalworking Cyclopes who, in fact, make the supernatural weapons that assure Zeus and his principal officers of their victory, and the hundred-hands who are then used by the triumphant Zeus as his jailers. And – whereas prison-officers need to be strong, and higher-ranking servants of the law, like Tyr or Scaevola, above all need to instill trust in their word – it is conceivable that these monsters have each received an additional ninety-eight hands, rather than losing one, to make them more fitted to their humbler duties.[7]

Therefore, it seems that the story of the Uranides is more archaic and more coherent than I was hitherto aware, and that, in a fanciful, fictional form, and with the alterations usual in traditions that no longer have any religious value proper, it preserves a complex system of representations, a whole interplay of concepts and symbols, an entire theory of sovereignty.

Conclusion

The analysis of couples conforming to the Mitra-Varuṇa type will have to be extended, no doubt, to areas I have not yet suspected. We already know enough about such couples, however, to be sure that this bipartition was very important. Enough, also, to define their limits and originality. And it is on these last two points that I now wish to lay stress.

Faced with certain tendencies in Indian thought, the reader might in fact have received the impression that oppositions of this type had a limitless field of application, that they constituted a method of division that could be used for all the concepts comprised in representations of the world. Seeing day and night (India, Rome) and autumn and spring (Iran) drawn into this classificatory current, some might have called to mind that fundamental couple found in Chinese classifications, *yin* and *yang*. And perhaps, indeed, the thought of the Indo-Europeans might well have found, in the facts we are dealing with here, both the material and the instrument for a Chinese-style systematization. In practice, however, it did not venture very far along that path. Even so, the comparison is an instructive one.

Marcel Granet (*La Pensée Chinoise*, pp. 115-148) has investigated the uses of the terms yin and yang in the earliest texts, those from the fifth to the third centuries B.C. and even that early their applications are very widespread indeed. They are found in astronomical, geographical and musical texts, and the "male-female" orientation is more than suggested. (The primacy of this last aspect is not very probable, however, since the two corresponding characters are formed with the *mound* radical, whereas any notion that is essentially, primitively feminine as opposed to masculine would contain the *woman* radical. It began to emerge very early, however, under the influence, Granet thinks, of hierogamic representations such as Earth-Heaven, Water-Fire and the like, which are so important in all Chinese speculation.) Whatever the origin of the words and their graphic representations, however, concrete universe and abstract universe alike were very quickly distributed between yin and yang. Points and segments of time and space, social functions, organs, colors, sounds, were all divided into antithetical dyads with the aid of massive or exiguous correspondences, of symbolic interactions, of mathematical artifice or dialectical analogy. And that, according to Granet's analysis, is the primary characteristic of this couple: it has no clear definition other than as a principle of classification, as a form of thought. Its material, the attributes it connotes, which are in any case limitless, are of less importance. It corresponds to a type of mind that pushes to the extreme the recognition and use of *contrasts.* A second characteristic is also common to at least a very large number of these contrasts: they are not only antithetical, they are also *rhythmic,* which is to say, subject to a system of alternations, of which the seasons provide the most typical natural example.

Perhaps I have not attached enough importance to this notion of rhythm in our Indo-European couples: the double alternation that constitutes the series of Rome's first four kings (the Lupercus Romulus; the king-priest Numa; Tullus, who reacts against Rome's "senescence" under Numa; Ancus, who restores the regime of Numa);

myths such as those of Othinus and Mithothyn, Othinus and Ollerus; the periodicity of the Lupercalia; the annual swing from the spring festival of Naurōz (Ahura-Mazdāh) to the autumn festival of Mihrjān (Mithra): all these facts, and several others, should be examined anew from this fresh point of view.

Similarly, the analogy with yin and yang frees me from the task of defining our Indo-European coupling exactly in terms of its material: it too, being essentially a mode of thought, a formal principle of classification, evades such definition. At the most, one can provide *samples* and say, for instance, that one of the two components (Varuṇa, etc.) covers that which is inspired, unpredictable, frenzied, swift, magical, terrible, dark, demanding, totalitarian, *junior*, and so on; whereas the other (the Mitra side) covers that which is regulated, exact, majestic, slow, juridical, benevolent, light, liberal, distributive, *senior*, and so on. But it would be futile to start from one element in these lists of "contents" in the hope of deducing the others from it.

Can the analogy be pushed any further? Did the "sovereign concepts" couple evolve, like *yin* and *yang*, toward a sexed interpretation, toward a "male-female" pairing? If we take the Indo-European world as a whole, it appears not. In Rome, Fides is a feminine divinity only because she is a personified abstraction, and she is so little opposed to *Iupiter* as female to male that she is in fact doubled with a masculine equivalent, Dius Fidius. In reality, within each of the two types of representations, there is room, should it be required, for both sexes, in which case the types of relations between the sexes are then radically opposed (the behavior of the Luperci toward the anonymous women they whip, as opposed to the holy and personal union of *flamen dialis* and *flaminica*, etc.). But the most precociously philosophical of the Indo-European regions, India, did indeed set out along the path of the sexed couple, and did so, it appears, like the Chinese, under the influence of their powerful hierogamic representation of heaven and earth:[1] is Varuṇa not "the other world" and also, albeit not in any stable way, heaven (cf. οὐρανός), whereas Mitra is "this world"?[2] But a fact that seems very odd at first glance, and contradicts the Chinese system (heavenly *yang*, earthly *yin*), as well as a Greek development (Uranos, the "male" of Gaia) – a fact doubtless to be explained by the passive character often taken on by what Mircea Eliade terms the "hierophanies of heaven" (*Dyauh*, "heaven" is, after all, constructed grammatically in many Vedic texts as if it were feminine) – is that it is Varuṇa who is endowed with feminine values, those of *yin*, and Mitra who takes on the powers of the male, of *yang*. The *Śatapatha Brāhmaṇa*, II, 4, 4, 19, says that "Mitra ejaculated his seed into Varuṇa" (*mitro varuṇe retaḥ siñcati*). The same *Brāhmaṇa* (XII, 9, 1, 17), though contrasting him this time with Indra as the male, confirms that "Varuṇa is the womb" (*yonir eva varuṇaḥ*). This sexual primacy of Mitra's, and this sexual impregnation of Varuṇa by Mitra, indeed link up nicely with Mitra's conceptual primacy and Varuṇa's conceptual impregnation by Mitra which are expounded, for example, in *Śatapatha Brāhmaṇa*, IV, 1, 4,[3] an important text in which Mitra and Varuṇa are successively opposed as the *kratu* (who formulates desire) and the *dakṣa* (who executes desire), as the *abhigantṛ* ("conceiver") and the *kartṛ* ("actor"), as *brahman* and *kṣatra* (more or less, as we say, "spiritual power" and "temporal power"). This text explains that Mitra and Varuṇa were once distinct (*agre nānevāsatuḥ*); but that, whereas Mitra (*brahman*) could subsist apart from Varuṇa (*kṣatra*), the reverse was not the case, and that, consequently, Varuṇa said to Mitra: "Turn toward me (*upa māvartasva*), so that we may be united (*saṃsṛjāvahai*); I assign you priority (*puras tvā karavai*)." In this light, I believe it becomes easier to understand the origin of certain concepts in later Indian philosophy. The *sāṃkhya* system, which holds the universe to be collaboration between a spectator "self" which it calls *Puruṣa*, "the male principle," and the *prakṛti*, an active, multiform, female "nature," felt that its *Puruṣa* and its *prakṛti* were antithetical in the same way as Mitra and Varuṇa (*Mahābhārata*, XII, 318, 39; *Mitram puruṣaṃ Varuṇam praktṛiṃ tathā*). In the other great Indian philosophic system, the Vedanta, the two antithetical components are *Brahmā* and *Māyā*, and they, too, are divided in accordance with the same system: on the one hand, the celestial projection – masculine – of the brahman (and remember that the old liturgical texts, when contrasting him with Varuṇa, say that "Mitra is the brahman"); on the other, the creative illusion (and *maya* in the Veda is the great technique of the magician Varuṇa). I leave historians of philosophy to evaluate these coincidences, and to decide whether they are mere chance or whether the two dualistic philosophies developed in part from the early myth of bipartite cosmic sovereignty. I have already expressed my opinion (*Flamen-Brahman*, appendix 1: *la carrière du brahman céleste*) that the concept of Brahmā the creator, of Brahmā taking himself as sacrificial victim at the beginning of time in order to constitute the world order, did not spring into being as the mere fancy of one thinker, but as an amplification and stylization of early rituals of human sacrifice, the purpose of which was the periodic renewal or maintenance of social and world order, and in which the victim was normally a terrestrial brahman. Similarly, it is also probable that the triads of "qualities" that played so large a role in Indian speculations are not wholly different in kind from the early theory of the threefold division of social and cosmic functions. Nor, indeed, is there anything exceptional in a myth that gives rise to a philosophy.

Yin and *yang* determine a general bipartition of the universe, at all its levels. Is the same true of the Indo-European pairing of sovereign concepts? Assuredly not, since, in the Indo-European system, sovereignty is only the first of the three levels of both universe and society, so that the dualist formula characterizing it is adapted to that level alone. It is quite true that the other levels, that of the warrior and that of the third estate, that of victory and that of prosperity, are also, either occasionally or regularly, presided over by paired divinities. For example, at the morning pressing of the soma sacrifice, we find Indra-Vayū on the second level juxtaposed to Mitra-Varuṇa, then the twin Aśvin or Nāsatya on the third (*Śatapatha Brāhmaṇa*, IV, 1, 3-5). But it is easy to establish that the intention, the stability and the inner mechanism of these dualist formulas are very different from those of the Mitra-Varuṇa coupling: far from being antithetical and complementary, the two Aśvin are interdependent and equivalent to the point of being indistinguishable; and as for the association of Indra with Vayū, it is merely one of the very numerous associations to which Indra is prone, associations that are so numerous precisely because they are the products of particular occasions and never make any profound inroads into the unitary, unipolar, solitary structure of the fighter-god. Of course, India would not be India if these straightforward analyses did not encounter an exception: the fundamental hierogamic representation, heaven-earth, has, on occasion, exerted its influence on these various couples: "the Aśvin are in truth heaven and earth," we read, for example, in *Śatapatha Brāhmaṇa*, IV, 1, 5, 16 (and even as early as *Ṛg Veda*, VI, 72, 3); but that does not entail any sexual consequence for them, one does not "ejaculate his seed" into the other, and they remain undifferentiated. In short, this fleeting assimilation has no more importance than when *Ṛg Veda*, I, 109, 4, invokes Indra-Agni as Aśvin, or (X, 61, 14-16) again assimilates Agni and Indra to the Nāsatya; or, again, when *Śatapatha Brāhmaṇa*, X, 4, 1, 5, interprets the Indra-Agni couple as the equivalent of the kṣatra-brahman couple. These are simply the customary and conscious games of Vedic "confusionism."

It will be interesting to confront the Indo-European mechanism isolated here with mechanisms other than that of *yin* and *yang*. Analogies will be found – as will differences, of which I can give one important example. One might be tempted to compare the "good" Mitra alongside the "terrible" Varuṇa with certain forms of messianism known in the ancient Near East, or with the great Christian dogma of the "son" as intercessor and savior juxtaposed to the avenging, punishing father. It does not seem, however, that any development in this direction was initiated in any region – except Iran, where Plutarch (*Isis and Osiris,* 46) was able to take Mithra as being a *μεσίτης*, a "mediator" (but, even then, a very specific type of mediator between the principle of good and the principle of evil), and which, above all, provided the Mediterranean world with the elements of "Mithraism," a salvation religion that proved capable of almost tipping the scales against Christianity for a period. But this particular development is doubtless to be explained by Iran's geographical position, its particular neighbors, and the probable contacts that resulted, at a very early stage, between its own religions and others that were centered around a suffering and triumphant savior. Moreover, it was a development that did not take on any precise form, significantly enough, until that moment when the religion of Mithra had in fact become detached from Iran.

Notes

Chapter One

1. Cf. the approval of this suggestion, which I was particularly heartened to receive, from P. W. Koppers, *Anthropos,* XXXII (1937), pp. 1019-1020, and *Mélanges van Ginneken* (Paris, 1937), pp. 152-155.

2. See A. Körte, *Argei,* in *Hermes,* LXXVII (1942), pp. 89-102.

3. Cf. Koschaker, *Die Eheformen bei den Indogermanen* (Berlin-Leipzig, 1937), p. 84, quoted by H. Lévy-Bruhl in *Nouvelles Etudes sur le très ancien droit romain,* 1947, p. 67. Also, P. Noailles, "Junon, déesse matrimoniale des Romains" (in the *Festschrift Koschaker,* I, p. 389): suggesting that the *confarreatio* might even be a form of marriage reserved solely for the flamines and rex.

4. *JMQ* I, p. 66ff.; *Revue de l'Histoire des Religions,* CXXXI, 1946, p. 54ff.

5. From the two lines of Ovid's *Fastes* (II, 21-22) I quoted, G. Wissowa (*Rel. u. Kultus der Römer,* 2nd ed., 1912, p. 517, n. 6; cf. Unger, "Die Lupercalia," *Rhein. Museum,* XXXVI, 1881, p. 57) has concluded that it was the rex and the flamen dialis who distributed the magical *februa* to the Luperci. It has been objected, however, that in Ovid's lines *februa* could refer to purifications other than the Lupercalia, since Varro (*De Ling. lat.,* VI, 3, 34), followed by Festus and Lydos, said that *februum* means *purgamentum* in general, and *februare* "to purify" in general. The objection is a weak one. This gen-

eral meaning must be an extension, as when we speak of "carnival" nowadays when referring to any kind of masquerade. In fact: (1) there is no trace of any use of *februum*, or of words derived from it, outside the Lupercalia; (2) the fact that the month of the Lupercalia is distinctively called *februarius* confirms that it was to those particular lustrations, indeed, that *februum* and its derivatives applied; (3) another passage from Varro himself (*ibid.*, VI, 4, 34) established the equation: *ego arbitror Februarium a die februato, quod tum* februatur *populus,* id est Lupercis *nudis lustratur antiquum oppidum Palatinum gregibus humanis cinctum* ("But I think that it was called February rather from the *dies februatus*, 'Purification Day,' because then the people, *februator,* 'is purified,' that is, the old Palatine town, girt with flocks of people, is passed through by the naked Luperci"); (4) when Servius (*Commentary on the Aeneid,* VIII, 343) says *pellem ipsam capri veteres februum vocabant* ("the ancients called that goatskin *februum*"), he cannot be referring to anything but the Lupercalia. Therefore, it seems that Ovid's lines, which occur, moreover, at the beginning of that book of *Fastes* devoted to February, do indeed refer to an early stage of the Lupercalia: at the outset of the rites, those responsible for social order perform a sort of "transmission of power" to the representatives of sacred violence.

6. Need I add that I have never claimed – as one critic inadvertently wrote – that the Roman Luperci were, in the first place, half-equine, half-human monsters?

7. Cf. the argument sketched out in the "Introduction" to *Servius et la Fortune*, pp. 15-25.

Chapter Two

1. At the very moment the first edition of this book was being published, M. Kerenyi was making an observation of the same kind in *Die antike Religion*, 1940, pp. 199-200, with reference to the flamen dialis, who is always clothed, and the naked Luperci.

CHAPTER THREE

1. Cf. *JMQ* III, p. 110ff. where this point is more clearly brought out by reference to Cicero's *De natura deorum*, III, 2.

2. Cf. *Tarpeia*, p. 164.

3. Cf. *JMQ* I, p. 189ff.

4. Cf. *JMQ* I, p. 78ff. (the magician Jupiter's technique of achieving victory contrasted with that of Mars, the warrior).

CHAPTER FOUR

1. For this list and the functional value of each of the gods that appears on it, see *JMQ* III, pp. 19-55, and my article to appear in the second section of the *Studia Linguistica* of Lund (1948): "Mitra, Varuṇa, Indra, and the Nāsatya as Patrons of the Three Cosmic and Social Functions."

2. I am delighted to be in agreement here, in essence and in many details, with Mr. A. K. Coomaraswamy, in his fine book, *Spiritual Authority and Temporal Power in the Indian Theory of Government* (American Oriental Soc., New Haven, 1942).

3. Which we must take care not to dissociate – as has been done recently – and to make use of separately, outside the system that gives them their meaning.

4. On *Vofionus* as the exact synonym of *Quirinus*, Benveniste, *Rev. de l'Hist. des Rel.*, CXXIX, 1945, p. 8ff.

5. Could this throw light on the enigmatic Irish *adaig* (**ad-aig*?) for "night"? But where does the final phoneme come from?

6. These admirable pages should be read in their entirety. I have attempted to develop other suggestions from them in *JMQ* III, p. 107ff.

7. Cf. also *Atharva-Veda*, XIII, 3 (addressed to the sun), stanza 13: "This Agni becomes Varuṇa in the evening; in the morning, rising, he becomes Mitra. . . ." For arguments against an inverse interpretation (Mitra as originally nocturnal) in India and Iran, cf. my arguments in *Rev. de l'Hist. des Rel.*, CXXIII (1941), p. 212ff.

8. Needless to say, this does not preclude other Latin texts from speak-

ing of *more Numae* in relation to animal sacrifices (*Juvenal*, VIII, 156).

CHAPTER FIVE

1. See *Tarpeia*, p. 196ff.

2. Cf. *Horace et les Curiaces*, p. 79ff.

3. Cf. *JMQ* III, ch. 2 and 3; M. L. Gerschel has also pointed out to me a significant linking of "Zeus" and "Helios" in Xenophon, *Cyropaedia*, VIII, 3, 11ff.; and 7, 3.

4. A curious lapse has led to these lines being taken as an admission that I am attempting to set up a jealously "comparative" method, in opposition to the "historical method" (R. Pettazzoni, *Studi et materiali di Storia delle Religioni*, XIX-XX, 1943-46, *Rivista bibliografica*, p. 7ff.). A close re-reading, however, will confirm that they simply draw a legitimate distinction between two problems, that of Mithra's *history* and that of the *vestiges* that subsist, within that history, from his *prehistory*. "Comparatist" in this context is merely a shorthand method to denote the scholar who is trying to reconstitute, like I am in this book, by means of comparisons, fragments of the religion of the Indo-Iranians or the Indo-Europeans. The same observation applies to the other passage in this book (see the section on Dius Fidius: "It is of little importance, etc...") which Signor Pettazzoni also uses, with no greater justification, for the same purpose.

5. *JMQ* III, p. 86ff.

CHAPTER SIX

1. I have never claimed that there was no other binding god in Greece than Uranos; or denied that Zeus, in other mythic groupings, was also occasionally a binder, and so on (cf. Ch. Picard, *Revue Archéologique*, 1942-43, p. 122, n. 1). I am simply saying that, in the dynastic history of the Uranides – which is a constructed narrative, and one of the rare pieces of Greek mythology that seems to me to call directly, genetically, for Indo-European comparison – the opposition, the *differential* definition of the two modes of combative action is clear-cut: Uranos binds, with immediate and infallible seizure;

Zeus wages a hard-fought war.

2. On the magico-legal symbolism of the "bond," see most recently H. Decugis *Les étapes du droit,* 2nd ed., 1946, I, ch. VI, "Le pouvoir juridique des mots et l'origine du nexum romain," p. 139ff. (p. 143: the binding gods; p. 157: the power of knots; p. 162: the *nexum,* etc.).

3. I hold to the contents of this section, even though it provides easy prey for specialists in Roman law. May it at least give them food for thought!

4. On the relations between the cow and both Mithra and Vohu Manah, cf. *JMQ* III, pp. 101, 133-134.

5. Cf. *Horace et les Curiaces,* p. 85ff.; V. Basanoff, *Annuaire de l'Ecole des Hautes Etudes, Section des sciences religieuses,* 1945-47, p. 133, and *Le conflit entre "pater" et "eques" chez Tite Live* (explication of the myth of the *transvectio equitum*), *Annuaire*... 1947-48, p. 3ff. And M. P. Arnold has just published a book entitled *Mavors.*

CHAPTER SEVEN

1. On another type of kingship, acquired by merit, see *Servius et la Fortune,* p. 137ff., p. 196ff.

2. *JMQ* I, p. 95.

3. Cf. n. 1, chapter six.

4. See some reservations relating to this negation in *JMQ* I, p. 252ff., and in *Tarpeia,* p. 221ff.

5. It is also the Latin *vultus.* Cf. also Illyrian personal names in *Voltu-* (*Voltu-paris, Volt(u)-reg-*): Kretschmer, "Die vorgriechischen Sprach- und Volksschichten," *Glotta,* XXX (1943), p. 144, n. 1. On *ullr,* see now I. Lindquist, *Sparlösa stenen,* Lund, 1940, p. 52ff., 179ff.

CHAPTER EIGHT

1. Cf. Rudolf Holsti's thought-provoking book, *The Relation of War to the Origin of State,* Helsingfors, 1913.

2. Cf. *Tarpeia,* p. 274ff.

3. L. von Schroeder, *Arische Religion,* I, 1916, p. 487, n. 1, has already

linked this Germanic *regnator omnium deus* with Varuṇa, lord of bonds, but, paradoxically, making *Tîwaz the beneficiary.

4. Cf. the original but rather unlikely solution offered by M. R. Pettazzoni in the *Atti della Accad. dei Lincei* (mor., hist., and philol. sc.), CCCXLIII, 1946, (Rome, 1947), p. 379ff. (expanding a thesis first propounded in an article in *Studi e Materiali di storia delle Religioni,* XIX-XX, 1943-46): it would seem that the problem doesn't in fact exist.

5. Cf. *Servius et la Fortune*, p. 230ff.

CHAPTER NINE

1. On the various Horatii heroes, cf. *Horace et les Curiaces*, p. 89ff.

2. Cf. *JMQ* I, p. 36ff.; *Horace et les Curiaces*, p. 61ff.; *Servius et la Fortune*, p. 29ff., p. 119ff., p. 125ff.; *JMQ* II, p. 123ff., and all of ch. 3 (*Histoire et mythe*).

3. In other words, although the "one-armed sovereign," Nuada, is king of the Tuatha De Danann, it is their adversaries who benefit from the legalistic exploitation of that mutilation. In turn, this throws into prominence another situation relating to the "one-eyed sovereign": the other leader of the Tuatha De Danann, Lug, is indeed "one-eyed" as we have seen, but he is so only for a brief period, of his own free will, while assuming a grimace with magic effects. Now, in the battle that is in the offing, Lug's *adversary*, the most terrible of the enemy chiefs (who is, moreover, his own grandfather, whom he will strike down), is "Balar (or Balor) of the piercing gaze" (*Birugderc*), who is authentically one-eyed, and whose power, entirely magical, is linked precisely to that physical disfigurement, which is itself of magic origin. Of his two eyes, the story says (section 133), one, habitually closed, sprang open only on the field of battle, when it shot death at those unfortunate enough to be struck by his gaze. And we are also told the origin of this fearful privilege: one day, when his father's druids were busy concocting spells, Balar came and looked through the window; the fumes of the brew rose so that they reached his eye. (Cf. A. H. Krappe, *Balor with the Evil Eye*, Columbia Univ., 1927.) All these facts seem to indicate that the Irish tradition hesitated, at some point, as to whether the one-eyed and one-armed couple (and

the advantages gained by the two mutilations) were to be placed in the Tuatha De Danann camp or in that of their enemies.

4. The epithet *Llaw Ereint* is applied to Lludd only in another Mabinogi, that of *Kulwch and Olwen*; but the same personage is certainly involved.

CHAPTER TEN

1. Cf. *JMQ* III, p. 86ff.

2. *Servius et la Fortune*, p. 186ff.

3. *Horace et les Curiaces*, p. 79ff.

4. *Tarpeia*, p. 176ff.

5. Cf. the formula that, from Vedic times onward, precedes so many ritual gestures: *devasya savituḥ prasave aśvinor bāhubhyām pūṣno hastābhyām "in the propulsion of the god Savitṛ, by the arms of the Aśvin, by the hands of Pūṣan!"* (see the index of *Weber's ed.* of *Taitt. Saṃh.*, and L. von Schroeder's of *Maitr. Saṃh*).

6. Cf. ch. 6, n. 1.

7. On the Cyclopes and the hundred-hands, cf. also *Tarpeia*, p. 221ff.

CONCLUSION

1. Cf. A.K. Coomaraswamy, *Spiritual Authority and Temporal Power in the Indian Theory of Government*, 1942, p. 50ff.

2. Certainly Indo-Iranian notions, and no doubt Indo-European: see Coomaraswamy, p. 85.

3. Translated into French by M.L. Renou in his *Anthologie sanskrite*, 1947, pp. 32-33.

This edition designed by Bruce Mau
Type composed by Archie at Canadian Composition
Printed and bound Smythe-sewn by Quebecor/Kingsport
using Sebago acid-free paper